D1406417

Media Flight Plan 7

A Strategic Approach
to Media Planning Theory and Practice
Seventh Edition

Printing 1.0

Dennis G. Martin, Professor Emeritus, Brigham Young University
Robert D. Coons, Media Research Director, Lowe Campbell-Ewald

ISBN: 978-0-6159882-8-3

Copyright Agreement

Important Software Notice

Acknowledgments

The authors express appreciation to the following for their professionalism and excellence:

Media Flight Plan Text & Workbook:
Jon Trelfa, Web Programming and Design
Virginia Martin-Rutledge, Chief Editor
David Spencer, Director Digital Media, Lowe Campbell Ewald, Digital Media Chapter & Exercise
Professor Jay Newell, Editorial Consultant, Iowa State University
Professor Daniel Stout, Surf Shoppe Case Study Author, Brigham Young University, Hawaii
Professors Amy Faulkner & Beth Egan, Syracuse University, Advisors, University Media Plan

MFP Online Simulation Beta Testing Consultants:
Sarah, Emilie, and Ashley Coons
Maiah G. Rutledge

To Gayle, the love and joy of my life,
who always believed in me even when I didn't.
And, to our children - Virginia, Callie, Denise, Adam, Alicia, and Ben.
Gayle, a true friend of the Academy,
cherished her friendship with countless professors,
and took great joy in attending the AAA conference every spring.
We miss you, Gayle, and appreciate all you did to help grow,
manage and develop Media Flight Plan.
~Dennis~

To Iris, my wife and companion,
our kids Michelle, Sarah, Erin, Emilie, Ashley, Spencer, Dan and Scott
and my parents Dale and Hazel
Love, Dale

Table of Contents

Section I *Media Flight Plan* Text Chapters

Section II *Media Flight Plan* Exercises

Section III *Media Flight Plan* Case Studies

Preface

Deer Creek Publishing has invested unprecedented resources into developing the first web-based *Media Flight Plan* software and textbook. Our seventh edition provides access to data from real-world syndicated sources including MRI, CMR, SRDS, and Nielsen data – all integrated online with exercises and case studies - and, as far as possible, presented in the same format found in the professional marketing/media world. Although change is inevitable with new editions, adopting professors have asked us to maintain the original *MFP* philosophy. That philosophy is first, to provide a text that encourages students to learn theoretical and applied principles of media planning. Second, to help students learn how to apply media theory intelligently and thoughtfully. And finally, to create software simulations that help simplify the complex world of reach curves, frequency distributions and media efficiency models.

Rapid change in the media world has increased the demand for more powerful yet user-friendly software. We are confident that we have made improvements consistent with the changing world of marketing and media planning without sacrificing simplicity or accuracy. At the same time, we have continued to provide emphasis on the fundamentals needed by practitioners in their daily work lives.

Despite technological advances, the authors believe the most valuable knowledge a student can take from studying this discipline goes beyond rote memorization of media terms, formulae, and rate book skills. The *Media Flight Plan* philosophy is to move students beyond mechanical application of media skills. A text such as this is designed to push intellectual boundaries, to encourage analytical thinking and rigorous problem solving. Students must learn to apply both theory and applied media principles intelligently. Following a series of text chapters and exercises, we conclude this text with a set of marketing intensive case studies. Together, all of these elements combine to deliver an integrated marketing/media planning experience.

When employers interview a candidate for an advertising or marketing position, more than any other quality they want a person who knows how to analyze and solve marketing/media problems. They want to hire individuals educated to think strategically. Moreover, they will insist on someone who knows how to articulate this strategy in writing. *Media Flight Plan* will continue to focus on strategic planning as the most important knowledge goal. When used as intended, *Media Flight Plan* helps eliminate busy work and focus student time and energy on marketing problem solving and strategic planning. While we may not succeed in simplifying all of the complexities of media planning, our goal is to deliver as much reality as possible while providing a real-world experience that blends the practical with both applied and theoretical knowledge.

Section I

Media Flight Plan
Text Chapters

BASIC MARKETING AND MEDIA LANGUAGE

A prerequisite for working with media research data is to have a command of the language and to learn the basic theory behind the language. First, however, you have to commit to learning the language. Sharing a common, precise language helps media planners, buyers, sellers, and researchers communicate clearly and effectively. As you work with the terms and concepts in this chapter, try to grasp *what they mean* instead of trying to memorize every detail. This will help with the formulas later in the chapter. First, learn the meaning – knowing what to do will follow naturally because you've got a basic knowledge of the concepts.

Universe (Population): A universe is the total group of persons in a specific geographic area that share a common characteristic. An example would be "Women age 18-49" or "Adults living in D counties." Universes have a geographic limit—*Total US* or *Detroit Metro*. Universes can be made of *Households*, and although *Households* aren't persons, they can be treated as if they are--any formula that works for a demographic group also applies to households. The terms *Universe* and *Population* are interchangeable—different research services use one or both. Universes are important—they are the basis for many calculations in the media world. Here is an example of the universes used by the Nielsen Company for their national television measurement service:

Estimates of U.S. TV Households and Persons in TV Households (Millions)#

	HOUSE-HOLDS	WRK WOM 18+	WOMEN 18+	18-34	18-49	25-54	35-64	55+	MEN 18+	18-34	18-49	25-54	35-64	55+	TEENS TOTAL 12-17	FEMALE 12-17
COMPOSITE	99.40	47.80	101.70	30.72	62.66	59.33	52.31	30.64	93.36	30.63	61.24	57.49	49.45	24.17	22.14	10.87
TERRITORY																
NORTHEAST	20.67	10.60	21.96	6.53	13.41	12.72	11.32	6.74	19.72	6.42	12.88	12.12	10.52	5.15	4.22	2.07
EAST CENTRAL	13.35	6.11	13.41	3.94	8.08	7.67	6.93	4.19	12.12	3.83	7.78	7.33	6.51	3.27	3.00	1.47
WEST CENTRAL	15.69	7.57	15.49	4.63	9.47	9.02	7.93	4.74	14.35	4.62	9.35	8.85	7.65	3.77	3.48	1.70
SOUTHEAST	19.61	9.36	19.90	5.82	11.88	11.28	10.15	6.36	17.86	5.67	11.38	10.73	9.39	4.95	4.18	2.06
SOUTHWEST	11.39	5.24	11.47	3.67	7.31	6.83	5.90	3.21	10.57	3.64	7.12	6.61	5.57	2.56	2.87	1.41
PACIFIC	18.69	8.92	19.47	6.15	12.51	11.81	10.08	5.40	18.73	6.45	12.73	11.85	9.81	4.47	4.40	2.15
COUNTY SIZE																
A	39.24	20.08	41.52	13.00	26.35	24.92	21.42	11.77	38.22	13.15	25.85	24.19	20.18	9.15	8.45	4.15
B	30.48	14.61	30.68	9.42	19.12	18.02	15.77	9.06	27.97	9.26	18.53	17.36	14.84	7.10	6.63	3.27
C&D	29.68	13.11	29.50	8.30	17.19	16.39	15.11	9.81	27.17	8.22	16.86	15.95	14.44	7.92	7.06	3.46
CABLE/VCR STATUS																
CABLE PLUS ADS	75.16	37.91	77.82	23.21	47.62	45.65	40.57	23.40	71.66	23.20	46.82	44.52	38.42	18.44	16.19	7.95
CABLE PLUS WITH PAY	47.53	25.98	50.66	16.11	33.07	31.79	27.54	12.79	47.75	16.07	32.67	30.79	26.50	10.73	11.58	5.69
BROADCAST ONLY	24.24	9.89	23.88	7.51	15.04	13.68	11.74	7.24	21.70	7.43	14.42	12.97	11.03	5.73	5.95	2.92
VCR OWNERSHIP	84.20	43.64	88.13	27.52	56.74	54.20	47.60	23.51	82.43	27.30	55.35	52.16	45.08	19.87	20.35	9.99
HHLD SIZE																
1	24.43	5.08	14.35	1.61	3.90	4.49	5.36	9.43	10.08	2.55	5.71	6.06	5.18	3.50	0.00	0.00
2	31.81	15.33	32.69	7.04	14.23	15.30	17.37	14.81	28.50	6.61	11.81	12.52	13.49	14.08	0.99	0.49
3+	43.16	27.40	54.66	22.07	44.53	39.53	29.58	6.40	54.79	21.47	43.72	38.91	30.78	6.59	21.15	10.38
4+	26.06	16.46	34.57	14.68	29.80	25.65	18.48	2.96	35.53	14.00	30.11	26.32	20.48	2.95	17.30	8.49
PRESENCE OF NON-ADULTS																
ANY UNDER 18	37.12	21.81	42.32	18.43	38.28	33.99	22.93	2.29	36.50	13.74	32.04	29.59	22.07	2.15	22.14	10.87
ANY UNDER 12	28.19	15.72	31.77	16.23	29.43	25.83	14.90	1.52	26.67	11.28	24.32	22.67	14.94	1.27	10.47	5.14
ANY UNDER 6	16.98	8.98	19.46	12.50	18.24	15.07	6.68	0.78	16.20	8.69	15.12	13.73	7.30	0.63	3.65	1.79
ANY 6-11	18.16	10.04	20.16	8.32	18.59	17.60	11.36	1.07	17.01	5.51	15.39	14.88	11.19	0.85	8.77	4.31
ANY 12-17	17.16	10.87	20.19	5.19	17.84	16.33	14.48	1.18	17.82	4.40	14.94	13.69	13.06	1.21	22.14	10.87
HOUSEHOLD INCOME																
$30-39,999	12.18	5.90	11.97	4.12	7.67	7.05	5.85	3.43	11.43	4.29	7.72	7.03	5.32	3.01	2.76	1.35
$40-59,999	19.60	11.62	20.35	6.90	14.11	13.43	11.30	4.53	20.85	7.31	14.74	13.96	11.48	4.47	4.98	2.44
$60-74,999	10.00	6.75	11.04	3.50	8.02	7.94	6.71	1.93	11.79	4.02	8.52	8.17	6.94	2.14	3.05	1.49
$75,000+	18.78	13.36	22.00	5.98	14.98	15.32	14.37	4.26	23.44	6.51	15.63	15.59	15.25	4.85	5.12	2.51

Universes can be added as long as they are *mutually* exclusive. Mutually exclusive means no part of the cells being added overlap. For example, add the 18-34 cell for Men and Women to get Adults 18-34.

You can also subtract cells as long as the cell being subtracted is completely contained in the cell it is subtracted from. Therefore, if you needed Women 50+, you could obtain that figure by subtracting Women 18-49 from Women 18+.

Impression: An impression is one *opportunity* for one individual to see an advertisement. If you are watching a television program, you have the opportunity to see any spots placed within it, or if you are reading a magazine, you have the opportunity to see the ads contained therein. *There is no guarantee a viewer, reader, or listener will actually be exposed to the ad.* This is an important concept to remember. Some audience members will miss all or part of the ad as they leave the room to get a snack, or flip over a large portion of a magazine to get to a particular item of interest.

Audiences to advertisements are rarely measured. Typically, it is audiences to media vehicles (i.e. individual programs or magazine titles) that are measured. Movement toward measurement of commercial audiences is being made in national television, but the industry is not there yet. Program commercial minute ratings are produced for minutes of a program that contain at least one second of a commercial, weighted by the number of commercial seconds--not exactly the same as 'commercial ratings', but much closer using program ratings as a surrogate.

Fortunately, since research studies are almost always done using "opportunities to see" as the measurement standard, research results can be transferred to the "real world" and understood in terms of the everyday media environment.

Exposure: An exposure occurs when a person "consumes" an ad. As noted previously, this is rarely measured. Doing so is problematic or prohibitively expensive in most cases, and since both media planners and researchers commonly use the impression standard, it's not an issue that affects trade. Exposure is sometimes used as a synonym for impression. Technically speaking, it is not. When "exposure" is used as a synonym for impression, think "exposure to the medium" and not "exposure to the ad."

Net Reach or **Reach**: A count of persons with at least one impression. The number of impressions received is irrelevant to reach; each person is only counted one time. Because that number doesn't tell the planner much by itself, it is most often expressed as a percentage of the *universe*. Here is the first media formula you'll need to know:

$$reach = \frac{\# \, persons \, reached}{\# \, persons \, in \, universe} \times 100$$

There is only one "requirement" for this formula, which is that all the numbers must be on the same "scale." You'll often see counts presented in research as thousands (000) or millions (MM or o'000), but for some media, like radio and cable, the numbers are often in units or hundreds (00). You may have to convert either reached persons or the universe into the measurement of the other in order to get the correct answer.

Reach is a flexible concept—it works for any demographic, including households. It also works for media schedules, campaigns, or individual programs or magazines. In any case, each person is only counted once—either they received an impression or not; and the persons counted as exposed must share the same unit base as the universe in order to get the correct reach. (Remember, exposed to the campaign or program, *not* to the ads).

Reach for an individual program, magazine, radio program, or other media vehicle has a special name. It is called a *rating*.

Rating: The portion of a demographic universe that is exposed to a specific media vehicle expressed as a percentage of that universe:

$$rating = \frac{\text{\# persons exposed to vehicle}}{\text{\# persons in universe}} \times 100$$

Ratings are usually rounded to one decimal place.

Ratings from different universes cannot be averaged, because the demographic universes used as denominators are different. To arrive at the correct Adult 25-54 rating from Women 25-54 and Men 25-54, you must convert the ratings back to persons for both demographics, and add them together. The total is divided by the sum of the universes. If the rating for Women 25-54 was a 5.0, and for Men 25-54 a 3.0, simple averaging would give a 4.0 rating. That is incorrect. Assuming universes of 10 million and 8 million for women and men 25-54 respectively:

10,000,000 x 0.05 (rating converted to decimal)	=	500,000
8,000,000 x 0.03	=	240,000
Total Impressions	=	740,000
740,000 / (10,000,000+8,000,000) x 100	=	4.1, the correct answer

The tenth of a rating point difference in this example may seem insignificant. However, you need to consider that hundreds of millions of dollars in media inventory are traded daily. Tenths of a point literally add up to millions of dollars.

You may discover other ways to correctly calculate combined ratings. For now, however, to avoid confusion we'll stay with a single method that we know will always work.

HUT, PUT, PUR, PUMM: These acronyms stand for "Households Using Television," "Persons Using Television," "Persons Using Radio" and "Persons Using Measured Media." All express a similar concept: the total number of persons (or households) using television (or radio) during a particular time period expressed as a percentage of the universe. PUMM is a special case of PUR, used in radio markets that are measured with meters. In those markets, only stations transmitting a special signal can be measured. When all outlets transmit the signal, PUMM is equal to PUR. These measures are used to get a sense of overall medium usage, and are often used by media buyers to forecast ratings for future time periods. Here are the formulas:

HUT= # households using TV during time period / total households in universe x 100
PUT = # persons usin g TV during time period / total persons in universe x 100
PUR = # persons using radio during time period / total persons in universe x 100
PUMM= # persons using measured radio during time period / total persons in universe x 100

These formulas work for any demographic universe.

Does the formula for HUT/PUT or PUR/PUMM look strangely familiar? It should—like "rating," these are also cases of "reach" that have special names. In essence, HUT is the reach of all television programs being aired during the same time period. PUR/PUMM is the equivalent for persons listening to radio.

Program ratings and HUT/PUT are related through a third measure, called *share*.

Share: Share indicates the portion of the available television (or radio) audience that is viewing a particular television program (or radio station). It is calculated this way:

share = rating ÷ PUT x 100

As with other formulas, the calculation is the same for all demographics. In the case of households, HUT is substituted for PUT, and if you're calculating a radio share, PUR (or PUMM) is substituted for PUT.

Shares are important because they help put ratings in perspective. Without share, planners and buyers might be misled to believe that "bigger is better." Programmers of television and radio networks would be tempted to cancel some strong programs based solely on ratings. In actuality some lower rated programs are outperforming programs with higher ratings. A "real life" example will clarify this idea.

During primetime, a popular program, *NCIS*, has a rating of 6.8. Later in the evening, *The Tonight Show*, with Stephen Colbert, has a rating of 4.2. Which is stronger? The answer is we don't know unless we see how well each draws from the available audience. The statistic that shows available audience is HUT/PUT (PUR for radio). And strength of audience draw is represented by share. It so happens that the primetime HUT for *NCIS* on the night in question was 69.7. HUT for *The Tonight Show* was 34.8. Calculating share for each, the winner is:

Tonight Show share	= 4.2 ÷ 34.8 x 100 = 12
NCIS share	= 6.8 ÷ 69.7 x 100 = 10

From these calculations, we see that *The Tonight Show* is doing quite well despite its lower rating. In fact, it's actually a bit stronger in its fringe-prime time slot than *NCIS* in prime. Figuratively speaking, *HUT/PUT represents the size of the available pie*, while *share represents the size of the slice. The Tonight Show* enjoyed the bigger slice.

Net vs. Gross

All of the terms defined thus far can be termed "net"—in each case a person is only counted one time, re-gardless of the number of times they are reached or exposed. It's sort of like counting the people who come to the dessert table or the bar at a banquet. Knowing the number of unique people at the bar or dessert table lets us know how many people were served in each location, but we still want to know how much beer or how many pies will be needed. That's because we all know people who make trips for seconds and thirds. Media planning is similar in that duplication occurs—some persons will have multiple opportunities to see our ad. Planners need to know how the "advertising pie" is being distributed—how many people are getting more than one slice, and ultimately how many media pies ("weight") should be put on the table.

Media concepts that include duplication usually include the term *gross* in the label. That's a tip-off that every impression is counted instead of every person. Let's extend the concepts we've learned so far and see what their duplicated partners are, and how all of them assist planners and buyers to analyze and see the whole planning picture.

Gross Impressions: The total number of opportunities to see provided by a campaign or plan. Remember that an impression is an opportunity to see an ad, and almost always represents the audience to a particu-lar program or magazine, not to the ad itself. In an ad campaign, multiple programs, magazines and other media opportunities are used—and many persons in the target audience have more than one opportunity to see an ad. The sum of all those opportunities is the total number of gross impressions. Gross impressions for a campaign or media plan often run into very large numbers. You'll often see Gross Impressions (abbreviated GI or GIMP) reported in thousands or even millions.

The term Gross Impressions by itself isn't terribly useful—and it's difficult to comprehend, since the numbers are so large. It's like asking you to imagine what a billion one dollar bills looks like—you know it's a lot of money, but most of us don't have experience that would allow us to visualize the concept of "billions."

Where are you most likely to run into Gross Impressions? Gross Impressions are commonly used is to calcu-late CPM, a relative measure of cost we'll see a little later in this chapter. Another (somewhat cynical) usage for Gross Impressions is in sales materials companies use to "wow" their suppliers and franchisees. The ob-jective is generally to impress clients with the amount of activity that is occurring by using 'boxcar' numbers (sometimes even to make a smallish schedule look bigger than it is).

Given the unwieldy nature of Gross Impressions, what do planners, buyers and clients use as a currency and descriptor of media weight? The answer is Gross Rating Points, which, as you might guess, is the "gross" counterpart of the "net" rating.

Gross Rating Points (GRPs): Gross Rating Points are commonly abbreviated in writing and in speech as "GRPs"—but can also be pronounced in humorous ways, the most common of which is "gurps." You might also hear "grips" depending on what area of the country you're in.

GRPs can be calculated several ways. We'll talk about a couple so you can see how various media terms are related. The first way is to divide total gross impressions by the universe and multiply by 100:

$$GRPs = gross\ impressions \div universe\ x\ 100$$

While this might look like the calculation for reach, it is different than reach because there is duplication involved. A person can be counted more than once, and many are. That is the reason that 100 GRPs is not the same as reaching 100 percent of the universe. Some will have been exposed to the campaign multiple times, some will only have received one impression, and some no opportunity for exposure at all.

A little algebra applied to the above equation demonstrates another basic GRP concept:

100 GRPs = a number of gross impressions equal to the size of the universe

1 GRP = a number of gross impressions equal to one percent of the universe.

So, for a demographic group of 20 million persons, 20 million impressions equal 100 gross rating points, and 200,000 gross impressions equal 1 GRP.

A common way to calculate GRPs is to simply add up the ratings of the media vehicles. Assume your target is Women 18-24. You buy 3 spots in a TV show with a 5.0 rating, and 2 spots in a magazine with a 4.5 rating:

3 spots	@ 5.0	= 15.0
2 insertions	@ 4.5	= 9.0
TOTAL		= 24.0 GRPs

Some important issues are implied here. First, *all the ratings summed together must have the same demographic base.* You cannot add Men 25-54 GRPs and Women 18-24 GRPs, just as you cannot add their ratings. And secondly, even though ratings are a "net" measure, when they are summed, they become "gross" (hence gross rating points). They are not equal to reach any longer because of duplication. This schedule produces 24 gross rating points, but may only reach 12 or 15 percent of the target audience.

TRPs (Target Rating Points): Are the same thing as Gross Rating Points. Some agencies use the term TRPs to refer to GRPs for a specific demographic, and reserve GRPs for households.

Average Frequency: Used to describe the average number of times a reached individual was exposed to a campaign (remember—exposure to medium, **NOT** an ad). It is calculated simply by dividing the gross impressions by the persons reached, or by dividing the gross rating points (GRPs) by reach:

average frequency = gross impressions ÷ persons reached
average frequency = GRPs ÷ reach

Here are two examples:

7,800,000 gross impressions ÷ 6,000,000 reached = 1.3 average frequency

300 GRPs ÷ 75 reach = 4.0 average frequency

One more reminder: All the values used *must* have the same demographic base. Rearranging the GRP/reach equation for average frequency, we see the most ubiquitous formula in the media world:

REACH x AVERAGE FREQUENCY = GRPS

Frequency Distributions, Effective Reach and Effective Frequency

Reach/Frequency models used at agencies to estimate the reach of media schedules also model *frequency distributions*. A frequency distribution simply lists the number of persons reached at each level of frequency. The techniques used to model this information are outside the scope of this discussion, but there are very good discussions of reach/frequency modeling that have been published[1].

Frequency distributions are generally used to understand *effective reach* and *effective frequency*, two concepts based on communication/learning theory. The idea is that repetition is required to "learn" or "remember" an advertising message. The level of repetition or frequency required is dependent on many factors, such as complexity of the message, clutter (level of advertising in general, and specifically competing messages), relevance, ad environment and others. When target audience members have received the appropriate level of advertising (i.e. the required number of impressions) the ad becomes "effective." This frequency level is called *effective frequency*, and the proportion of the universe exposed at that level is called *effective reach*. The model below shows a frequency distribution for a schedule of 100 GRPs in primetime TV for Adults 25-54. **The "F" column means exactly this frequency level, and F+ means exposed this many times or more.**

	F	F+
0	54.7	100.0
1	20.8	45.3
2	10.8	24.5
3	6.0	13.7
4	3.4	7.6
5+	4.2	4.2

Some programs use "N" or "X" instead of "F". This example shows figures in percentages. You can see that the total reach of the schedule (persons reached one or more times) is 45.3%. If we had determined that the effective frequency level was "two or more times," then the effective reach for this schedule would be 24.5%. Setting an effective frequency level is as much art as science. There are numerous methods for estimating this level in use at different agencies. Most are based on the judgment of the research group.

You should be aware that many ad agencies lean toward a different view of advertising, often referred to as "recency theory[2]." This model places far less emphasis on frequency, and emphasizes exposure close to the sale. In fact there is convincing evidence for this model, especially with consumer products. Because the effort is directed toward placing impressions close to the sale, continuous advertising to as many people as possible becomes more important. Continuity is important because different people are continuously coming to market. And reach is important because pinpointing different individuals coming to market is difficult.

Media Costs and Comparisons

As planners and media buyers start looking at various media options, the issue of performance comes up— how to get the most "bang for the buck." Many things must be considered when planning or buying media. For example, will the vehicle environment (sitcom vs. drama; beauty column vs. food column, etc.) affect the communication objectives? Are the sight, sound and motion of television, the thought-evoking capabilities of radio, or the luxurious appearance of an upscale magazine the best environment for telling the story?

Such questions will be set aside for now — these are strategic considerations discussed in other parts of this textbook. Although these and other considerations are taken into account in real-life analysis, cost comparisons must be made.

It's difficult to tell if a program with a 5.0 rating costing $130,000 per spot is a better or worse buy than two 2.0 rated programs costing a total of $118,000. To make such comparisons easily, planners and buyers commonly use two measures, *cost per thousand* and *cost per point*. Both are essentially the same statistic. What makes them useful is that they put disparate sums of money onto a common cost basis.

Cost Per Thousand (CPM): The cost of delivering 1000 gross impressions. Cost per thousand is calculated by taking the total cost of a schedule, dividing that amount by the total impressions and multiplying by 1000:

$$CPM = total\ cost\ (in\ dollars) \div total\ gross\ impressions\ x\ 1000$$

Example: Two magazine insertions cost $45,000, and produce an estimated 4,000,000 impressions. They are combined with a radio schedule costing $10,000, and producing 2,500,000 impressions. What is the CPM of the schedule?

Total cost = $45,000 + $10,000 = $55,000
Total gross impressions = 4,000,000 + 2,500,000 = 6,500,000

Substituting: CPM = 55,000 ÷ 6,500,000 X 1000 = $8.46

Cost Per Point (CPP): Cost per point is the cost of one gross rating point. Its calculation is similar to CPM. Take the total cost of the schedule and divide by the total gross rating points:

$$CPP = total\ cost\ (in\ dollars) \div total\ GRPs$$

Using this formula, we can answer the earlier question of which program option was a better buy, 5.0 GRPs for $130,000 or 4.0 GRPs for $118,000:

$130,000 ÷ 5.0 GRPs = $26,000 CPP

$118,000 ÷ 4.0 GRPs = $29,500 CPP

Mathematically, the 5.0 rated show is a better buy. However, it's quite possible the other shows would be bought based on other criteria, such as the quality of the audience or appropriateness of environment.

CPP and CPM are related in the same way that GRPs (gross rating points) and gross impressions are related—through the universe that is common to both. They are basically the same measure. If you know the universe, you can easily convert from one to the other:

CPP = (CPM X Universe) ÷ 1,000   and...

CPM = (CPP ÷ Universe) X 1,000

For both of these formulas, the universe must be in units (not thousands or millions).

So which is best? The answer is neither. The one you will use depends on what information you have, or client/buyer preference. In practice, CPPs are most often used for broadcast media, while CPMs are used more frequently for print.

Additional Print Terms
There are a few additional terms you should be familiar with when dealing with print media. While these concepts could be applied to other media, they are most commonly used with print.

Composition: Composition refers to the "make-up" of a magazine audience. It is calculated by dividing the desired demographic audience by the total audience of the publication, then multiplying by 100:

$$Composition = target\ audience \div total\ audience\ x\ 100$$

A magazine with 250,000 "Women with children" readers and a total audience of 2,000,000 has a "Women with children" composition of 12.5%:

$$250{,}000 \div 2{,}000{,}000 \times 100 = 12.5\%$$

Composition is used to find publications that are "popular" with a particular group—in other words, which magazines have the highest *concentration* of the target. While most commonly used with magazines, the concept of composition can obviously be applied to other media.

Circulation: Is simply the number of copies distributed by a publication. It is a measure of absolute size. Planners use circulation analysis to understand the overall health of a publication, and to find publications with certain characteristics, such as those with circulation emphasizing a particular area of the country. The Audit Bureau of Circulation (ABC) audits circulation statistics for consumer magazines. Individual publications pay to have their circulation audited.

Coverage: This media term is usually used in connection with newspapers. It refers to the portion of households in a market that are in the publication's delivery area. Because newspaper readership varies widely from market to market, buyers frequently buy newspapers to reach a particular coverage level in a market.

Coverage can be confusing because it also has other meanings. When used with magazines, for example, it really means 'rating'. And with television programs, it means the percentage of households that are in markets where the program is broadcast.

Internet Terms

Relatively speaking, the Internet is a "young" advertising medium. It has many attractive characteristics, such as high targetability, and interactivity. Because of its unique character, unique measures have been developed to adapt advertising to the Internet. As measures become more formalized and better defined, industry groups are moving the Internet measures toward measures used in other media. Impressions are the primary measure for web planning, although it is possible to estimate ratings and GRPs with some services.

In order to understand current Internet measurements, it is necessary to consider the basics of how users navigate the Internet. Navigating the Internet is accomplished via a *browser*. Browsers are programs that display web pages.

It's all about the files. Whenever a web page is visited, a file is loaded. Each icon on the page, each ad, and each other element is displayed via a file request embedded in the page. Each link to another page is nothing more than a request to load another file. This brings us to the first Internet measurement, *hits*.

Hit: A request for a file. It is probably obvious now why this measurement is no longer used to measure web audiences. Each file request on a page results in a 'hit' on the host computer; some pages contain numerous hits, others just one or two.

Page Views: The number of times a page is completely delivered to a browser. This is quite an improvement over hits—each page is counted once as a unit. Although an improvement, page views still do not tell us anything about the individuals who viewed them.

Impressions: The delivery of an ad to a browser. There are various means employed by ad delivery services to determine if an ad was delivered. However, delivery of an ad does not mean a consumer viewed it. In this respect, it is similar to the previous definition of an impression—an opportunity to see.

Other Internet Measurements

All of these measures are derived by looking at computer logs. Their strength is that they are all objective physical measures. Their weakness is that they don't tell us anything about the person seeing the page or ad.

That kind of information is available from syndicated research services that use survey panels to follow web viewing habits of participants.

Participants in these panels load tracking software on their computer. They also give the research company information about themselves, such as age, gender, household income, and other characteristics. The software asks users of the computer to log in when connecting to each session of web surfing. The respondent's surfing activity is monitored by the software, which reports the activity back to the research company where it is aggregated with information from other panel members and reported to subscribers of the service.

These panels measure the activity of individuals, other statistics are available for web sites, and in some cases, individual web pages. Some of the statistics may include:

Unique visitors: Analogous to reach. This is the estimated number of unique persons that visited a particular site. Various demographic breaks are available depending on the service.

Usage statistics: Syndicated web research services also provide various measures of usage, such as time spent per day or month and average number of page visits. These are fairly self-explanatory and vary by service.

Social Media and Word of Mouth Measurement
Measurement of social media and word-of-mouth are still in their infancy--much like the Internet was ten years ago. While there is plenty of evidence advertisers can have effective communication with consumers using these media, measurement is less well defined than other media.

Summary
In this chapter you've learned a number of important terms and concepts that will help you in your everyday work, whether for an agency or corporation, advertiser, or medium. These terms, formulas, and theoretical models form the basic currency on which all media are analyzed, bought and sold.

These are not all the terms you will use in your marketing or media planning career. However, if you understand these well, you will have a solid foundation to build on. You'll also find that as you encounter these new terms, they will logically follow from these building blocks.

Endnotes

[1] See, for example, Sumner, Paul, *Readership Research and Computers* 1985 Newsweek International; Greene, Jerome, *Consumer Behavior Models for Non-Statisticians: The River of Time* 1982 Praeger.

[2] For information on recency theory, see Jones, John Phillip, *When Ads Work* 1995 Simon & Schuster.

MEDIA MATH CONVENTIONS

Clients, planners, buyers and others are used to seeing media figures reported in specific ways. You should learn and use the "common language" of these reporting conventions:

Ratings: 4.5, not 4.5%. Ratings are not written with a % sign, even though they are percentages with one decimal place. The one possible exception to this rule are cable ratings, which are frequently carried to two decimal places because they are so small.

Reach: 78.3, not 78.25673 or 78.25673%. Reach is also written without a % sign, even though it is also a percentage, and rounded to a single decimal place--more than that is just silly given the margin of error inherent in the data.

Average Frequency: 2.8, not 2.83744. Again, just one place will do nicely.

(oo): this is the way to indicate the numbers are in hundreds. Usually used with radio audiences and universes.

(ooo): indicates the numbers are in thousands. M after a number also means that the number is in thousands. M is the Roman numeral for 1000

MM: MM after a number means millions (M x M, or 1000 x 1000). To convert a number in millions (MM) to thousands (ooo), shift the decimal place three places to the right. Ex: 11.23 MM = 11,230 (ooo)

GRPs (Gross Rating Points): are written as whole numbers (e.g. 324 not 323.8), especially in a document that goes to a client.

CPM (Cost Per Thousand): is a cost. Don't forget the $ sign (e.g. $12.35 CPM)

CPP (Cost Per Point): is a cost. Remember the $ sign, and round to the nearest dollar (e.g. $12,000)

DIGITAL MEDIA

Digital Media: A New Age in Advertising

The youngest generation knows no different, but for most generations, digital technology has transformed the way people think, behave, and live. Consumption of media has become widely fragmented with the introduction of the Internet in the 1990s, mobile phone devices in the early part of the 2000s, and tablets in the later part of the 2000s. These swift advancements in technology have provided virtually unlimited opportunities to reach consumers in new ways and the advertising community has been continually challenged and excited by the possibilities.

The Digital Ecosystem – An Increasingly Complex Space

There are nearly 1 billion active websites, over 2 million mobile apps, and nearly 500,000 tablet apps in the world today. To add to the complexity, consumers move seamlessly across devices when accessing the content they seek. As a result, advertisers must create plans that reach their targets agnostic of device. Aside from location-based targeting and in-app advertising which are exceptions that are exclusive to mobile and tablet devices, most concepts related to planning and buying are similar across digital services. Location-based targeting will be covered later in the chapter.

Nielsen Online and comScore are two major syndicated resources that provide audience data for users across desktop, mobile, and tablet devices in the United States. You're familiar with the Nielsen name as a measurement service that provides ratings for television. These resources help advertisers make sense of audiences across devices and identify the best advertising opportunities to assist in developing a Digital Media plan. Syndicated services such as comScore and Nielsen Online provide at a minimum count data (impressions) for digital media, but many also provide demographic and psychographic insights as well.

Developing a Digital Media Plan - Where do we begin?

There are four key steps involved in developing a digital media plan: target definition and behavior, digital media objectives, simplify, and select.

1-Define your target - There are two important components here. The first is the overall demographic and psychographic makeup of your target. This component is built using a combination of syndicated and primary research to define typical profiles of your best prospects (For more on targeting, see the chapter *Marketing Driven Media Plans*). Included in this first step is a better definition of the primary digital media channels typically used by our target (e.g., heavy users of tablets, watch TV online, use search engines to research products).

Second, understand how your target behaves within each digital media channel. comScore and Nielsen Online will help inform this component. Various reports provide indexes for user digital behaviors (e.g., gaming, sports, email, social media, online video) against any target audience. These indexes help guide us when it comes time to determine the most appropriate digital media channels. (See the exercise *Using Indexes to identify Target Audiences* for more discussion).

Below is an abbreviated comScore report that provides some top line information on digital usage. This report shows about three quarters of online adults (76.8%) used social media sites in the past 30 days. We'll learn more about how to calculate various statistics later.

PLAN METRIX CONSUMER TARGET PROFILE REPORT

Country: US-Plan Metrix
Universe: Home and Work
Months: October 2013
Report Generated: 12/9/2013

comScore
© 2013 comScore, Inc.

Items 1 to 4 of 4 First | Prev |Next | Last	Base		Column 1			
	Target Audience (000)	% Vertical	Target Audience (000)	% Vertical	% Horizontal	Index
Age						
18+ yrs old (Total Audience)	181,628	100.0	25,416	100.0	14.0	100
Used social media sites in last 30 days						
Yes (Used social media sites last 30 days)	139,480	76.8	19,580	77.0	14.0	100
# of video streams watched on avg. day						
1-5 (video streams on avg day)	69,669	38.4	10,694	42.1	15.4	110
Video Games						
Yes - Played video games (offline/last 30 days)	70,294	38.7	10,359	40.8	14.7	105

2-Define your digital media objective – To develop good objectives, start with the end in mind: What are you ultimately trying to accomplish? At this stage in your planning process, the overall media objectives will have already been determined. At some agencies, the digital objectives are developed by the planners, others have a dedicated team that works primarily with digital media. The digital objectives may be the same or different than the overall media objectives, but should certainly be consistent with the overall goals of the advertising. Here are some common examples of digital media objectives:

- Raise awareness of a new or existing product
- Achieve a certain reach of your core target audience
- Drive engagement with your brand
- Drive a specified action on your site or social property (e.g., join a contest, use a store locator, download a file, sign up for a newsletter)
- Grow your social media following
- Enable customers to advocate on a brand's behalf
- Drive sales of your product (online and/or offline)
- Cross-sell new or different products to existing customers

Typically the digital media objective includes some combination of the objectives above. Depending on your final objective, there are different ways to approach your digital media strategy. The next step is to look at how we might select from the nearly limitless digital opportunities to meet the digital objectives.

3-Simplify the complex digital ecosystem—Now that we understand what we are trying to accomplish, we need to consider all of the advertising possibilities within the digital ecosystem. It is nearly impossible to cover all the digital opportunities available—indeed, new opportunities are created all the time. The following list is typical of primary digital media channels available today and a description of the advertising opportunities available within each:

Display Advertising

Visual ads that appear on a publisher website or mobile site next to and/or around publisher content (e.g., news, entertainment, blogs, sports, home and garden, shopping) and allow users to click through to the advertiser website. These were the very first ads in the digital space and are still prominent today.

Mobile and Tablet In-App

These visual ads appear in mobile or tablet device applications, and allow users to click through to advertiser mobile/tablet optimized sites or download the advertiser app.

Streaming Video / Pre-Roll

Pre-roll video ads appear prior to a user accessing publisher video content. Although some advertisers will simply run their 30 second television spot, it is much better practice to create shorter 10 or 15 second spots to run in the digital space. Consumers tend to consume more short-form content (vs. traditional television long-form content) and therefore have significantly less patience for 30 second video ads. Further, research suggests that the shorter ads do as well as longer ones, and even allowing viewers to skip ads after the first few seconds provides good advertising communication—viewers skip ads they've seen many times or that are not relevant, but view ads for products or services they are interested in.

Streaming Audio

Streaming audio services (e.g., Pandora, Spotify, Live365) run ads within streaming radio content.

Paid Social

Text and photo ads appear in or next to a user's content feed (e.g., Facebook News Feed, Twitter Feed).

Gaming

There are two typical forms of in-game advertising:

Dynamic – Dynamic ads are inserted into game elements as a user plays in a live gaming environment (e.g., a server might place a beer ad on a billboard in a street racing game in Microsoft Live). These ads are primarily branding and are typically not clickable to an advertiser's website. Dynamic ads are more easily placed and less expensive than hard-coded ads.

Hard-coded – Advertiser messaging or content built into the actual game that can be seen when a user is playing in an online or offline environment (e.g., Michelin tires available in a racing game). These ads are never clickable to an advertiser's website. Hard-coded ads usually have a high 'up front' cost and must be planned well in advance, as content is literally programmed into the game. One advantage is that hard-coded content 'lives forever'—it will be seen whenever the game is played.

Consumer Review / Directories (i.e., the "new" phone books)
Listings of business locations and display advertising in and around directory listings (e.g., YellowPages.com, WhitePages.com). In many cases there are consumer comments and reviews within the same environment (e.g., Angie's list, YELP).

Location-Based Targeting
Advertisers use the physical location of a consumer's mobile device to deliver advertising in the form of display ads, listings, or pop-ups (e.g., offering a coupon to a consumer in a store or a health drink display ad to a consumer that has visited a health club in the last 10 days). This method is often referred to as 'geo-fencing'—a virtual fence is placed around specific locations and advertising is delivered to devices that enter the fence.

Direct Email
Mass emails containing exclusively advertiser content sent to a list of targeted individuals. This is often referred to as an 'email blast' or 'blasting'.

Paid Search
Text ads that appear above and next to "organic" or "natural" search results across all search engines (e.g., Google, Bing). Organic results are those found by the search

engine that are related in some way to the terms that were searched. They come up 'automatically' as they are found by the engine.

Paid search ads are placed on the same page as the organic results, but are given the premium positions at the top and right of the page where they are easily seen. Advertisers can 'buy' search terms—ones they think are appropriate for their ad to appear next to. Sometimes advertisers even buy competitor brand names as search terms so they appear as an alternative to the sought for brand. In this screen shot, the page search ads are boxed to identify them.

4-Select the Right Channels – How do we craft a solid plan? We can use a combination of our defined digital media objectives and our defined target audience to determine the best digital media channels to help reach our goals. A third consideration in selecting channels is the size of the media budget. However, it is often useful initially to assume that money is no object.

It can be helpful to define roles for each channel by aligning them with a simplified advertising funnel. Keep in mind that these roles are not mutually exclusive (i.e., any channel can work towards achieving any objective), but the following chart identifies each channel's *core strength*.

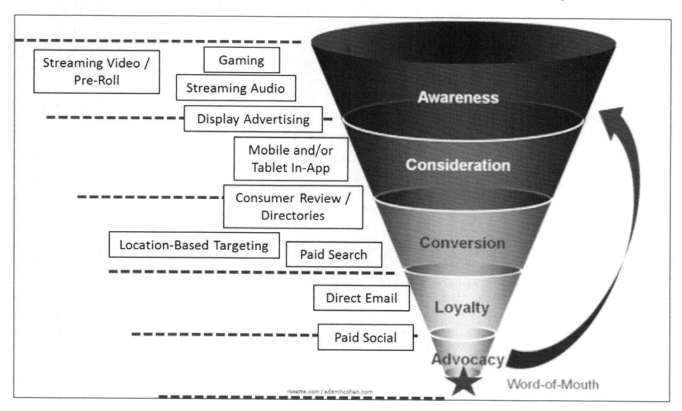

Now that we have an understanding of the core strength for each channel, let's examine how target audience behavior and tendencies will ultimately affect channel decisions. Reports from online measurement companies can demonstrate how engaged the target audience is with each channel. Recall that indexing is often used to identify audience behavior. Indexes above 100 inform us that our target audience is more likely to engage in a particular behavior than the "base" population (often adults 18+).

Likewise, indexes below 100 indicate that our target audience is less likely to engage in a particular behavior. Given a digital media objective of raising awareness, a report might show the following category indexes against our target audience:

Activity	Index
Watch video online	175
Participate in gaming online or offline	140
Listen to music online or on your mobile device	210
Read news articles online	95

Based on this data, our target audience is most likely to listen to music online or on their mobile devices (210 index) and least likely to read news articles online (95 index). Both streaming audio and display ads on news sites are great for raising awareness ("core strength" funnel), but we are much more likely to reach the target audience by placing an audio ad on an online music property than we are by placing display advertising on a news site. Taking it a step further, a more detailed report like the one below informs us that Pandora and Spotify are stronger offerings (with indexes of 148 and 142 respectively) against the target than, say, Yahoo Music or MSN Music (112 and 78 respectively). Pandora and or Spotify might be the first properties we add to the plan. Whether we added one or both would depend on such things as budget, the value of the deal, need for reach or the need to control frequency, whether added value items such as research were part of the deal, and so forth.

⊙ comSCORE

Key Measures
Entertainment - Music [Undup.]

©2013 comScore, Inc

Geography : United States
Universe : Home and Work
Time Period : November 2013(3 MO. AVG.)
Target : Persons: 25-34
Media : Entertainment - Music [Undup.]
Date : 12/10/2013

Media	Total Unique Visitors (000)	% Reach of Total	Target Unique Visitors (000)	% Reach of Target	Composition Index UV
Total Internet: Persons	224,998	100.0	34,657	15.4	100
Entertainment - Music	110,772	49.2	21,538	62.1	126
VEVO	24,226	10.8	5,222	15.1	140
PANDORA.COM	22,551	10.0	5,127	14.8	148
IHeartRadio Network	19,490	8.7	3,743	10.8	125
Spotify	15,972	7.1	3,498	10.1	142
Yahoo Music	16,299	7.2	2,823	8.1	112
MSN Music	9,273	4.1	1,119	3.2	78

Calculating and Reading Indices

As with other indices we have seen, indices for digital channels are a quick means of comparison between properties and channels, and are calculated in a similar fashion:

$$\frac{Percentage\ Reach\ of\ the\ Target}{Percentage\ Reach\ of\ the\ Base\ (Usually\ Total\ Internet\ Population)} x\ 100$$

Pandora example:

$$\frac{14.8}{10.0} x\ 100 = 148$$

While the 148 is technically a percentage, the percent symbol is commonly left out and no decimal places are shown to make the result easier to read. In this case, the target of adults 25-34 is 48% more likely to visit Pandora than the general internet audience.

Once a working plan is in place, it is often refined using estimates of reach and frequency. The major measurement services provide the tools we use to calculate the reach and frequency of the target across the different properties in a plan. Some are even able to provide unified estimates across mobile, search, and other elements of a digital plan. Publisher selection often changes at this stage as the planner works towards the reach and frequency goals for the target audience within the budget.

The Deal - We know what we want, how do we buy it?

"Robot or Human?" This is an important question to consider when buying digital media. There are a multitude of methods advertisers use to buy their digital media, involving different degrees of human intervention and automation. Here is a summary of three common methods:

> Publisher-Direct – The deal is negotiated directly with the websites. By using this method, advertisers can sponsor specific areas of a website that are more endemic to the brand, negotiate special "takeovers" (i.e., ownership of all advertising on the page), gain access to premium inventory (e.g., top ad on the website homepage), or sometimes even have the publisher create content on behalf of the client.

> Ad Networks – An ad network aggregates inventory across thousands of online and mobile publishers. As mentioned at the beginning of this chapter, there are hundreds of millions of active websites. It would be impossible for an advertiser to reach out to so many publishers. Ad networks allow an advertiser to buy an entire category of lifestyle interest and run ads across several similar websites. Going back to our earlier example, we know that gaming indexes well against our target. By using an ad network, we can buy advertising across 30 (or more) gaming sites with a single buy. Ad networks are typically more cost-efficient and help to maximize reach by expanding advertiser presence across so many sites.

> Agency Programmatic - "The Robot" – Publisher inventory is bought and sold in an automated marketplace. Billions of impressions of unsold publisher inventory (banner ad placements) are essentially put up for auction on what's called an "ad exchange." The model is similar to working with ad networks, but eliminating the middle man. Think of it like the active stock market where stock brokers are bidding against each other for the right to buy different stocks. Advertisers are bidding against each other for the right to buy a single impression on a website.

Measurement and Performance – How are we doing?

Digital media are unique from other forms of media in that the performance of a campaign can be monitored once it is set live. If you discover certain components of your plan are not working midway through the campaign, you can make changes. Changes to campaigns 'on the fly' are common, and can be done programmatically or manually. The process of continually analyzing and changing the site mix to improve performance is referred to as 'optimizing' a digital campaign. Results from previous campaigns can also be very helpful in guiding digital media decisions for future campaigns.

Chapter 2

Most advertisers use a set of metrics call Key Performance Indicators (KPIs) to measure and evaluate their plans. Here are some common KPIs and formulas for how to calculate:

COMMON KEY PERFORMANCE INDICATORS(KPIs)		
KPI	**Calculation**	**How Used/Commnets**
Click-Through-Rate (CTR)	$$\frac{\text{Total Clicks} \times 100}{\text{Total Impressions}}$$	CTRs are usually small, less than 1 percent (0.2 to 0.3 is considered average). The higher the CTR, the better the site is at driving traffic to the target website.
Action Rate	$$\frac{\text{Total Actions} \times 100}{\text{Total Impressions}}$$	An 'action' can be any measurable activity, such as filling out a form, requesting information, downloading a file or app, making a purchase, etc. High action rates indicate that the quality level (i.e., interest) of traffic is high. Averages range from 2 to 10 percent, depending on the simplicity of the action.
Conversion Rate	$$\frac{\text{Total Conversions to Sale} \times 100}{\text{Total Clicks}}$$ Or $$\frac{\text{Total Conversions to Sale} \times 100}{\text{Total Impressions}}$$	Depending on the denominator, high conversion rates show either more effective advertising (clicks) or more effective websites (impressions). Averages range from 1 to 5 percent using clicks as the denominator and .003 - .005 (three to five hundredths of a percent) when using impressions.
Video Completion Rate	$$\frac{\text{\# Completed Video Spots} \times 100}{\text{\# Delivered Video Spots}}$$	Typically used for pre-roll ads that run before video content is displayed. Can be an indicator of sites that have compelling content (people are willing to watch your ad before they get to see what they actually came for). VCRs tend to decline as the length of your ad increases. Average is around 70 percent.

COMMON KEY PERFORMANCE INDICATORS(KPIs)		
KPI	**Calculation**	**How Used/Commnets**
Cost-Per-Click (CPC)	$\dfrac{\text{Total Cost of Impressions}}{\text{Total Clicks}}$	Measure of *efficiency*. The lower the cost, the better. This KPI identifies websites that deliver clicks inexpensively. Typical CPCs range from 1 to 4 dollar range.
Cost-Per-Action (CPA)	$\dfrac{\text{Total Cost of Impressions}}{\text{Total Actions}}$	Related to action rate, but identifies websites that deliver actions efficiently. CPA depends highly on product category in terms of what is an acceptable range. For instance, a $100 CPA may be considered good for a $10,000 product, but highly unacceptable for a $20 product.
Cost-Per-View (CPV)	$\dfrac{\text{Total Cost of Impressions}}{\text{Total Video Views}}$	Typically for pre-roll video campaigns. Measures how efficiently a website can deliver views of your ad. Averages range from $0.02 to $0.25.

<u>Privacy and Consumer Data Protection – A Final Note</u> – Consumer privacy and protection of information in advertising has always been a priority for the Federal Trade Commission (FTC). The "Do Not Call" List is perhaps its most well-known initiative which provides consumers an opportunity to put their phone number on a list to prevent telemarketers from calling.

In the digital space, the FTC created the "Do Not Track" List allowing consumers to opt-out of tracking of online behaviors for advertising purposes. However, this initiative has had great difficulty in gaining the same kind of traction as the "Do Not Call" list. Currently, there are no official regulations or penalties for companies or advertisers that violate these rules. There is also a lot of debate in terms of the level of risk in targeting online behaviors as the majority of information advertisers use to target against is not "**P**ersonally **I**dentifiable **I**nformation" or "non-PII" for short. It is a topic of much interest in the advertising world as it would drastically reduce advertisers' ability to target consumers effectively if any legislation were to be enacted.

SOCIAL MEDIA, SOCIAL MARKETING AND ETHICS

A long-time friend of the author with over a million airline miles shared the following about her disappointing flight on Singapore Airlines. This happened several years ago just as Twitter became wildly popular. Here's her story:

> On such a long flight to Singapore, I felt lucky to get a bulkhead seat with lots of leg room, but my luck ended there. A couple of hours into the flight, the carpet got soggy with "blue water" leaking from the lavatory just behind the bulkhead. The plane was full with no spare seats. An exceptionally sympathetic flight attendant did her best to soak up the moisture, but it wasn't possible to eliminate the unpleasant odor. It got so revolting that I returned my dinner to the flight attendant in one of those little white bags.
>
> After landing, I didn't have time to stop at the ticket counter to register a formal complaint. Returning to Changi airport for the flight home, I explained my ordeal and hoped they would be considerate enough to offer a seating upgrade. The ticket agent called her manager, made a weak apology, and said, "Sorry, cannot. No upgrade possible." While waiting to board, I tweeted: **Stinky blu H2O under foot 17 hrs Sing Air to SIN. Returning SFO ask for comp to first class. Agent says sorry no upgrade for you. Really?**

Her twitter followers included a newly minted, female Delta captain. After landing in SFO, she was greeted by the Delta pilot's tweet: ***So not like Sing Air. You deserve more than "Sorry" for holding your breath 17 hours. Write to CEO.*** My friend said she appreciated a sincere expression of sympathy, especially coming from an airline professional. Another traveler tweeted, ***"Sorry you had to sit in pee for 17 hours. No upgrade for you speaks volumes."*** Who knows how many hundreds of fellow travelers may have shared her story, and to this day she avoids Singapore Airlines whenever possible. Not surprisingly, Delta gets most all of her international business. A little humanity and sympathy goes a long way.

Despite Singapore Airline's reputation for excellent service, one oversight by one employee can boomerang and create a snowball effect that goes far beyond one unhappy customer. Such is the power of social media in a time when every customer must be viewed as a future advocate or a flaming critic. Marketers are learning to treat customers like royalty, because they now have the power of kings and queens in the realm of social media.

Cultural impact of social media . . . is the medium the message?

Our traveler to Singapore illustrates how social networking has impacted the culture in ways few could imagine a decade ago. Far more than a trend, digital devices are saturating the culture, and social networks are shaping the way people connect with each other and the brands that define them. The way brands are perceived is also evolving as the medium shapes and alters the environment we live in. Perhaps more than any traditional medium, social media epitomizes the notion that the medium itself is the message.

Impacting communication theory in the 1960s, author Marshall McLuhan constructed a paradigm around the notion that "the medium is the message." Simply put, he proposed that the essence of a medium embeds itself in the culture and in the message, and actually becomes the message. Put another way, one might say that social media illuminate the message itself, and in turn influence the message. As McLuhan wrote, the medium, "like a light bulb creates an environment by its mere presence." (McLuhan, Understanding Media, pg. 8) To frame McLuhan's theory in the context of social media, as we use Instagram, for example, we tend to focus on the content (the stream of photos), but in the process, we largely miss, "the structural changes in our [culture] that are introduced subtly. . . " (Federman, M. 2004, July 23). Put more simply, as the fish is unaware of water as its medium, so are we unaware that increasingly, technology is the medium we swim in.

Social media defined: It's more about being social, less about selling.

Lowe Campbell-Ewald's Dale Coons, Director of Media Planning/Research and coauthor of Media Flight Plan, notes that, "Social media continues to expand; it's a media phenomenon with a 'big bang' effect in the advertising universe. For the foreseeable future, social media budgets will continue to grow and be a significant part of media and marketing efforts."

Sites like Twitter, Facebook, Pinterest, YouTube, and Instagram are only the tip of the social media iceberg, and no doubt you can think of another dozen off the top of your head. When new media emerge, advertisers move quickly to capitalize on them. Although there are countless ways to interpret social media, this definition goes to the heart of what it means to live in a socially constructed media environment:

> *Social media is a paradox for advertisers because it is a gossamer thread easily broken by excessive promotion. Social media should not be seen as just another advertising medium; at its core it is a two-way conversation. Compared with traditional media that delivers messages to demographic targets, social media engages human beings in civilized conversation.*

The power of creative social media

College students are among the most enthusiastic and prolific users of social media. Hopefully those interested in pursuing a career in marketing communications will not only learn from some of the best practitioners of the craft, but also set goals to be even more creative and more daring as they take the reins and reinvent this powerful medium.

The following article by Ed Keller is reprinted from MediaBizBloggers.com. We include part of his article to illustrate the power of creative social media, and to show that creative thinking and writing is vital to the future of this highly competitive medium.

Samsung was the sponsor behind Ellen DeGeneres's headline grabbing, record breaking, Twitter busting

"selfie" at the Oscars. For Samsung, it was part of a much larger, longer-term march to become one of the most talked about brands in America.

For quite a number of years running, Coke was the most talked about brand in America. Beginning in 2010 Apple started a sharp ascendancy and by Q4 of 2012 it had overtaken Coke. Samsung's WOM is rising rapidly, as well, breaking into the top 10 in 2012 and into the top 5 in 2013. (Source: Keller Fay's Talk Track®)

Samsung's WOM (Word Of Mouth) not only grew sharply during the past two years, but especially during the all-important holiday shopping season. Samsung's WOM increased by 150 million word of mouth impressions during the 2013 holidays versus 2012, while Apple's dropped by 359 million (more than any other brand).

No other brand has seen such a sharp rise in WOM as Samsung. How have they done it and what does the future hold? In terms of the quality of those conversations, both Samsung and Apple enjoy very favorable word of mouth. However, Samsung's sentiment improved significantly year-over-year (2013 vs. 2012) while Apple's net sentiment score declined. As a result, Samsung now enjoys a more favorable ratio of positive to negative WOM than Apple. With evidence that positive WOM drives sales, this bodes well for Samsung. (Source: Keller Fay's TalkTrack® 2013)

Samsung has succeeded with a twin strategy of delivering great product experiences while also successfully leveraging marketing communications channels. Marketing communications channels are more likely to be cited in conversations about both Samsung and Apple versus the average brand, although Samsung has a modest edge over Apple with 31% of Samsung WOM referencing ads, versus 28% of Apple WOM and 26% for the average brand. Samsung also holds an advantage when it comes to point of sale being more talked about -- 15% of Samsung conversations reference things people see at POS versus 12% for Apple and 11% for the average brand.

Samsung also has proven adept at creating WOM based on people's positive experiences. This is the heart and soul of word of mouth: When people's experiences are so motivating that they want to tell others, it creates conversations that are more persuasive and more likely to lead to sales. Whereas the average across all product categories is that 20% of conversations are sparked as a result of people's experiences with a product, for Samsung it is 32% -- two thirds higher than the norm – with Apple close behind at 29%.

Samsung's selfie at the Oscars brought together a wide variety of stars -- Ellen DeGeneres, Brad Pitt, Julia Roberts, Meryl Streep, Bradley Cooper and more -- all of whom were genuinely enthusiastic about being part of the picture. Similarly, Samsung's marketing strategy is leveraging a huge variety of tools from the major marketing groups of paid, earned and owned media. Samsung's success shows how powerful all those tools can be when used in an integrated and creative way. (From: Beyond the Oscars' Selfie: Samsung's Chase to Displace Apple as America's Most Talked About Brand -- Ed Keller -- Published: March 20, 2014 at 5:30 AM PDT) Ed Keller, CEO of the Keller Fay Group, has been called "one of the most recognized names in word of mouth.". Follow Ed Keller on Twitter, Facebook and Google+, or contact him directly at ekeller@ kellerfay.com...)

Advertisers have little if any control over the customer's messages

There is no guarantee that Samsung's impressive rise will continue, mainly because their biggest competition, Apple, has the experience, the technology, the brains and the treasure to remain king of the hill. Apple is no doubt keenly aware of Samsung nipping at their heels. All the big players have learned that there is an inherent danger in social media, i.e., advertisers have no control over the customer's messages. To remain competitive, Apple, Samsung, and hundreds of other national and local brands are not only investing in social media space, they are hiring creative teams who actively monitor social conversations about their brand, and responding to them in a way that capitalizes on positive conversations like the Samsung Oscar selfie.

Likewise, they do their best to turn negative experiences into positive communications by meeting the needs of disgruntled consumers. Travel and Leisure relates a story from Virgin Airlines, a company that carefully manages social conversations. "One customer had a hard time flagging down a flight attendant to pre-order a meal," says Abby Lunardini, a spokesperson for the airline. "After she tweeted about it, our team sent a message to the crew and she was served immediately." With consumers ensconced in social media, marketers now swim in the same fish bowl with their customers. Get it? The medium is the message. Heads up to advertisers: The consumer is no longer an isolated individual; she's part of a vocal community and has the power to make or break your brand in a tweet.

Consider that a majority of marketers, national and local, waste over half of their social media budget selling and promoting their brands and services at the expense of sociability. The be-all and end-all of social media is to remain loyal to the word "social." If your social media strategy is focused on selling and promoting, you are wasting most of your money.

Follow 80/20 rule – We See Ourselves as Social, Tribal Creatures, Not Targets

The authors suggest a ratio of 80/20. No more than 20% of social media content should be perceived by your audience as "advertising," and preferably 10% or less. Moreover, all products and services may not be a good fit for social media. The question each brand must ask is: Does my product fit into a social space that welcomes conversation?

Picture a social circle where people pull up a chair and engage in interesting conversation. Would people willingly join your circle if you hammer them with advertising and promotions? The secret to successful advertising in social media is about engaging people in a conversation that evokes ideas and feelings; it's much less about selling, much more about sharing.

Tillamook provides a good example of "socially engaging" social media. Tillamook is an Oregon based co-op owned by a group of over 100 dairy farmers. Their ad agency, Leopold Ketel & Partners, spends a significant share of their budget developing conversations with people who enjoy real dairy butter, prize-winning cheese, and a product their web site calls "creamy, dreamy" ice cream.

What could be more socially engaging than a Tillamook Ice Cream Social? A group of bloggers in Sacramento, California met for an evening of food and fun. They blogged, "we did it, well, because we are social, tribal creatures and need each other." Tillamook provided the goodies for a local contest engaging a group of professional bloggers. Someone at the party Instagramed, Favorite flavor of the evening: Fireside S'mores.

The photo featured Fireside S'mores. Another blogger tweeted, "It was shipped from Tillamook, Oregon especially for the event. Many thanks to Gillian, Kelly, and Katie for traveling from Tillamook to Sacramento and putting on what was virtually a mini blog conference. Thanks also to the Tillamook brand ambassadors who parked the 'Baby Loaf' VW van on the sidewalk and represented it with enthusiasm and pride."

Although the Tillamook brand is clearly visible among the dozens of photos for this event, 80% of the communication, photos and conversation, was about people enjoying "ice cream social experiences." People enjoyed sharing experiences about food and convivial life. Social Media managers should follow this key principle: navigate your brand's personality to fit naturally into social life. Natural social platforms build relationships and human conversation. At all costs, avoid advertising that pretends to be social media.

Content Is King: Trends suggest more job opportunities for communications graduates as more brands become publishers

Digital media strategist Lisa Talia Moretti is confident that marketers will start to take content a lot more seriously and view it as a fundamental first step towards launching a successful social media presence. There will be far fewer rookie errors of signing up to a social media channel without knowing what you'll be saying in that space. Assuming this trend continues, content budgets will grow and more brands will start to work as publishers. The result: marketers and ad agencies will need to hire more copywriters, editors and journalists in the process. It's not just about quick wins on YouTube anymore. It's about implementing long-term plans on how to inspire, educate, and entertain your community with content that best represents your brand's personality and keeping your message high on social content, low on promotion.

With the focus firmly on crafting words/images/videos, Moretti thinks our ideas about measurement will also evolve. More sophisticated metrics will begin to emerge like trying to understand how we audit the output of our content so that it becomes a barometer on trust, authority and advocacy. The authors believe reliable estimates for reach, frequency and other metrics are not too far off as this platform approaches $10 billion annually.

Blunt Competitors' Social Media Strategies in Your Next Media Plan

Social media marketing & intelligence continues to gain in relevance as businesses can no longer afford to tentatively treat social media as the weak division within their marketing channels. Nor can they allow themselves to fall behind the competition's social media efforts.

Jolanta Friss is a Facebook specialist (find her on Social Hunter (@JoaFriis). She writes extensively about online marketing and offers an intriguing look into the future. She asserts that social media offers a rich source of marketing and competitive intelligence information.

Beyond managing your own social marketing and media planning, she warns that competitors social media needs to be analyzed. Are you checking out your competitors to make sure you are not only matching their social media strategies, but planning to out-perform their marketing/media efforts? Analyzing your competitors' social media strategies and content will allow you to map the sources and rhythms of your competitor's online releases. With the right insights into what other brands are doing, you can improve your own media planning and social media content to gain market share and blunt your competitors' social media strategies.

Online Social Media Sites Essential in Many Media Plans

Friss also notes that social networking is increasingly requisite in the recipe for a successful media plan. Combine this with the fact that mobile devices are expected to exceed the human population in a year or two. Planners can't ignore it; for many products and services, mobile is a quintessential advertising and public relations medium. Social media platforms such as Facebook, Twitter, Google+, and YouTube have become indispensable in the media planners' tool box. Whether your campaign is national or local, effective social media strategies are no longer optional for most products and services.

Examples of Social Media Successes

Over the course of the last decade, an array of viral marketing examples have come and gone with varying

YOU CAN STILL DUNK IN THE DARK

degrees of success. Though the term "viral" infers that the campaign is organic and self-replicating, marketers and big-name brands have begun to attempt manufacturing viral content in the hopes of increasing their brand awareness or product sales. Some feel that viral content cannot be manufactured and is only the product of organic and unpredictable forces. However, a growing number of others feel that they can predict what people will be interested in, how they will share that content, and ultimately what will become viral. Though the debate rages on, the fact remains that viral marketing has evolved over the course of the last decade from a rather obscure Internet phenomenon to a massive, multi-million dollar marketing tool employed by agencies and brands the world over. Below we cite a few of the better examples of viral marketing in the last decade.

"You can still dunk in the dark," said the tweet heard 'round the world during the 2013 Superbowl blackout. It was the ultimate example of a brand using social media to spark a conversation. It lit up the Twittersphere by responding to real-world happenings in real-time. And it's exactly the kind of thing social media marketers need to be doing: They need to anticipate what their audience is going to be talking about, and then get in on the conversation immediately.

McDonald's may not have the best Twitter track record, but they got it right when Al Roker overslept for the Today Show. McDonald's tweeted him a picture of their McCafe latte with the note, "Stick with us @AlRoker, we'll help you wake up for the next 39 years #McCafe".

With its ear to the ground listening for social chatter about its brand, Smart Car USA picked up this tweet: "Saw a bird had crapped on a Smart Car. Totaled it." Smart Car USA responded quickly with a clever infographic showing how many bird poops it would actually take to total one of their cars (4.5 million pigeon poops, in case you need to know). As a result of its efforts, Smart Car USA got loads of Favorites and retweets, all because someone on the social media team was tuned into brand chatter.

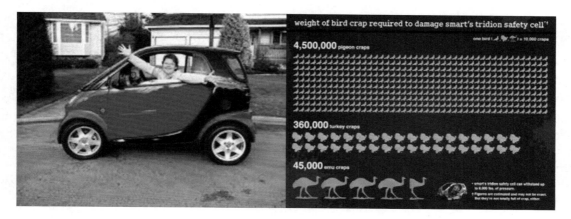

This ad by Dove titled "Evolution" was one of the first of a series of self-esteem related ads released to the Internet. The short 75-second clip generated more than 44,000 views within its first day of

release, more than 1,700,000 views with the first month, and more than 12,000,000 views within the first year. The ad is especially noted for the amount of discussion it generated on such broadcast television shows as "The View," "Good Morning America," and "The Ellen DeGeneres Show." It has been estimated that the clip has generated more than $150 million worth of "free advertising" due to its editorial exposure. It is emotional, clean, beautiful, and considered by many to be a classic. (If you're interested, Google "Dove Evolution.")

Marketing, Communication, and Ethics – The Trinity of Effective Social Networking

As marketers open the door wider and wider to social media, they must be aware that this medium exposes them in ways like no other. Ethics or lack thereof cannot be hidden in a social media fish bowl where corporate decisions are often exposed and become transparent. Consumers will 'call out' both successes and failures, and they express both with passion. As social media becomes more embedded in the culture, companies must learn to communicate both socially and ethically. They must act as fellow human beings who belong to a community, responding to consumers' needs in a 'golden rule' manner--putting the needs of consumers ahead of profits. When social media raises a red flag for a brand, failure to respond quickly and honestly may not only result in unnecessary deaths and billions in corporate payouts, but also loss of confidence and possible demise of a brand.

One pundit blogged that new-car showrooms might as well install revolving doors, as it seems the industry recalled nearly as many vehicles for safety reasons as it sold this year. Although as collective consumers we are exposed hundreds of brands daily, the majority rarely if ever result in social media backlash due to ethical breaches. Since most of us buy cars, we have come to accept that sooner or later most of us will get a recall letter from Ford, GM, Toyota, Honda, VW, et al. All five of these brands have issued safety-related recalls in the past three years. For example, GM issued a major recall for faulty ignition switches – which could turn out to be serious. Prius models had steering troubles. Honda Pilots, Odysseys and Acuras also had faulty ignition switches. Even exotic, expensive brands like Rolls-Royce, Lotus and Lamborghini had at least one recall since 2012.

A Case Study in Social Media . . . Driving Ethical Behavior

According to an ABC news report filed by Joseph Rhee in 2010, attorneys suing Toyota claimed that internal company documents showed that the automaker was able to confirm cases of sudden unintended acceleration that did not involve driver error. According to the suit, "Toyota failed to disclose that its own technicians often replicated Sudden Unintended Acceleration events without driver error." For an extended period, Toyota executives claimed floor mats were the only problem. Social media played a big role in changing public opinion about this.

A story filed by USA TODAY reporter Chris Woodyard (March 2014) lit up the twittersphere when he reported that Toyota agreed to pay a $1.2 billion settlement to resolve lawsuits alleging "unintended acceleration" in some Toyota and Lexus models. Toyota also admitted to wrong doing and paid the largest fine in US history for what Attorney General Eric Holder called "criminal wrongdoing." He announced, "We can say for certain that Toyota intentionally concealed information and mislead the public about the safety issues behind this recall." At least one industry analyst says the settlement is proof that Toyota was culpable. "Automakers don't pay billions of dollars to get rid of litigation involving driver error," says Sean Kane of Safety Research & Strategies.

Effective Social Media Demands Ethical Marketing. Instead of acting ethically when safety concerns were rife on Facebook and YouTube, Toyota officials hedged. Imagine the profits and good will lost by tweets like this from @CaptStephen: "Toyota president said: We grew too big too fast. Big and fast is not the issue--honesty and integrity is. Obviously [Toyota] is still hedging." Consumers hold a megaphone in social media. Brands must act so this voice is used in their favor, not against them. Toyota lost both faith and face by thinking they could hide from ethical, responsible communications.

As brands communicate honest experiences, consumers receive communication they can believe in, and something they value. But consumers won't continue to share in the brand's conversation unless the social marketer resonates honestly with their needs and expectations. In a world networked and dominated by customers who have the power to build or break a brand, brand managers should worship the holy trinity of effective social networking by consistently practicing Ethical Marketing Communications.

Putting Social Media in Perspective

Lest the reader get the impression that social media will soon flatten the world of traditional advertising, don't hold your breath. In Darwinian fashion, advertising as an institution continues to evolve according to its own kind of natural selection. Even as social media becomes a major medium, mutations are inevitable, and traditional media is far from an endangered species. TV and print advertising content are always evolving and adapting to other forms of distribution. Keep in mind that they are not beholden to a TV screen or two dimensional paper. Their content can morph into new shapes and sounds distributed via Samsung's Galaxy, Amazon's Kindle's, Apple's iPad, countless mobile phones. Show up at this year's CES (Consumer Electronics Show) and see tools already imagined, be they home based, even more highly portable or transported through nano tubes into 3-D holograms.

Audience metrics are still a challenge in social media. Compared with traditional advertising - which has had many decades to evolve its measurement techniques - social media measurement is still young. Despite the advantages of trust and intimacy inherent in social media, the advertiser faces limitations in evaluating social media. This medium is still working on new methods of measuring effectiveness.

Advertisers are well aware of the power of Twitter or Facebook via anecdotal evidence; however, there is no standard of measurement yet that can reliably estimate or predict the size of that audience. While social media imbues advertising with intimacy and communication power, traditional advertising maintains advantages that it has always enjoyed: the ability to 'get the word out' with broad reach. Despite limitations, advertisers are already learning to make good use of social media as it settles into its place in the media and cultural landscape.

MARKETING DRIVEN MEDIA PLANS

A marketing driven media plan recognizes that most media decisions are subordinate to marketing objectives and strategies. All advertising decisions, whether creative, positioning, or media strategies, will be much more effective when firmly rooted in marketing intelligence. The media planner must become thoroughly familiar with all available marketing facts that drive the media plan.

What is marketing intelligence? It is the discovery and evaluation of all promotional and marketing facts relating to the product – and fitting them to the media plan. *Media Flight Plan* software assumes all of your decisions will be justified with thorough marketing intelligence. This chapter provides a checklist of seven questions to help you prepare marketing-driven case studies for *Media Flight Plan* software.

SWOT (Situation Analysis): A Marketing Checklist For Media Planners
A SWOT analysis is essentially a situation analysis; it's an acronym that represents four elements of the process: **S**trengths, **W**eaknesses, **O**pportunities and **T**hreats. Whether you call it SWOT, Statement of Facts, or Situation Analysis, the seven points in this chapter will help you gather intelligent marketing information.

This list covers more questions than you will be able to research for most products. It would be wasteful of your time, and whoever reads your SWOT if you try to answer every question below. Focus only on *relevant questions that relate to your product*. Also, *avoid writing strategic recommendations or setting objectives when writing your SWOT*. The SWOT is a statement of facts – it *does not set any goals* or recommend actions.

Most of these questions deal directly with marketing, not media issues. However, a few questions will hit directly on media issues – these are to help you make the connection with marketing. Many researchers get inspiration for marketing ideas (strategies/objectives) while conducting this research. It's smart to jot down ideas for goals as you write the SWOT, but *save them for the media objectives/strategies section of your plan*.

1. Analysis Of Marketing Objectives & Strategies
A media plan must be consistent with the goals set for marketing. For example, assume a brand manager sets a goal to double current sales using a direct marketing television promotion. A media planner would need to know such goals so she could respond with an appropriate media plan. Consider these basic questions:

- The 4 P's: Product, Price, Place, Promotion. What effect do they have on the media plan? Uncover as much relevant information about these four pillars of marketing as you can.
- What is the total size of this market?
- What methods have been used to sell this product?
- Has advertising been used in the past? How? Which media?
- Where is this brand in the product life cycle? If this is a new product, developing awareness may be your highest priority. If product is mature, and competition is strong, reminder ads with higher levels of frequency may be called for.

- What are the sales goals for the product?
- Current share of market? Share goals?
- Current awareness for brand? Awareness goals?
- Is marketing budget available?
- Geographic breakdown for sales?
- Creative concept: Does it require a specific media mix? Social Media? SEO (Search Engine Optimization)? Are print media needed? Broadcast? Internet? Event marketing? Sales promotions? Demonstration? Is your concept highly memorable? If not, is media budget adequate to support high frequency to get awareness needed?

2. Competitive Considerations

A media planner needs to know as much as possible about the marketing and media activities of competitive brands. Suppose a competitor is spending double the amount in mass media compared to your brand. Moreover, all of it is being spent in broadcast media. This may leave open an opportunity to out-spend the competition in internet. Or, it may suggest the need to concentrate marketing dollars in just a few major markets where you can match competitive spending. Ask these questions:

- Who are all the major competitive players?
- What share of market do they have?
- Compared with competition, is your brand unique or is it very similar to competitors?
- How much is the competition spending?
- Which media does the competition use? Which vehicles?
- When do major competitors spend most of their money?
- What kind of sales promotion does the competition employ?
- Non-traditional media and guerilla marketing – do your competitors paint outside the lines?

3. Creative History Of Brand

Consider a situation where you are assigned to develop a media plan for Demae, a new chain of sushi bars located in California, Nevada and Arizona. Research reveals that 60% of prospective customers, adults 25-34, perceive Demae's fare as a healthy alternative to high calorie lunches, especially during the hot summer months. The campaign follows from these facts—the summer campaign positions Demae as a healthy, yet pleasurable lunch alternative. The campaign theme: "Tuesday's Lunch Special: 300 Low Tempura Calories!" How might this affect media decisions? First, it may help decide the media mix. For example, it may be effective to reach prospects right before or during the noon hour. Awareness of the creative concept should help you later when you need to write the media mix strategy. Consider the following questions:

- How is the product currently positioned?
- What is the current copy theme? Slogan? Headlines?
- Which media are currently being used by this brand?
- Is this product high or low involvement? If involvement is medium to high – the prospect is willing to invest time to gain knowledge about the product, and has considerable interest in the consequence of the purchase. Media should be considered that allow enough copy to provide details, e.g., magazines, Internet or newspapers. If involvement is low – product is purchased on impulse or with very little time investment – radio, TV or outdoor may be effective media choices.
- Make a list of benefits and specific qualities of your product, including psychological benefits. For example, in the case of the Demae Sushi bar, benefits might include: Fresh seafood, low fat, low calorie, fresh vegetables, and no artificial flavors. Guilt-free indulgence is a clear psychological benefit.
- How do users feel about the brand? Attitudes? Lifestyles?

- How is the product/service used? Consumed? When?
- What percent of budget should be considered for national media? Spot media?

4. Target Audience

It is vital to develop both demographic and psychographic target profiles. Many products appeal to multiple groups. If your product has wide appeal, assign a value to each group. It is always useful to conduct primary research (focus groups and/or surveys) to develop an accurate target profile. *When writing case studies, be sure to check mediaflightplan.com for syndicated data and other materials provided for the case. These may include data from MRI (Mediamark Research Inc.), TNS-MI (Competitive Media Reports), SRDS, and other companies.*

5. Geography Questions

It is important to know whether a brand is distributed nationally or regionally. If distribution is national, it's important to know if sales potential varies by metro markets or by region, and which regions hold greatest promise. It would be rare for a brand or category to be equally strong in all geographic parts of the country. Also, simply because a brand is distributed nationally, distribution alone is hardly adequate justification for spending media dollars in national media. Analyze all available marketing data, and then make a judgment call. Whether you advertise in national media only, spot media only or both, geographic strategy is critical to the success of your brand. Don't be afraid to take a risk as long as you can present a strong case based on hard marketing data.

- Is brand distributed nationally, regionally, or both?
- Advertise in national media only? Can this strategy be justified with quantitative marketing data? Remember that national buys cover all markets, including any spot markets under consideration.
- Advertise in national media with heavy-up buys in key spot markets. Does data support this decision?
- What percent of budget should be considered for national media? Spot media?
- Advertise only in key spot markets? Does available quantitative data support a spot market only campaign?
- Which spot markets have the best potential? Rank markets by EV% (see chapters on factor spreadsheets), and then divide them into subgroups of 5 or 10. Justify each group of 5 or 10 based on available advertising budget and other data.
- If you conduct a spot only campaign, how many markets will your budget handle? This may require trial and error buys on *MFP* (adding a few markets at a time). Can you penetrate enough markets (% of population or % of target population) to keep brand sales strong?
- The above assumes doing a spreadsheet analysis of all spot markets, ranking them top to bottom.
- What is BDI (Brand Development Index) and CDI (Category Development Index) for each major market?
- What types of non-traditional media can be justified in national or spot markets?
- Does guerrilla marketing hold potential for this brand? Nationally? In spot markets?
- What percent of budget should be considered for non-traditional media? Which media?

Approach all of these questions based on marketing facts. For example, on the question of national budget, you could write: Possible allocation: Split budget 70% national and 30% spot. Spreadsheet analysis indicates that 18 spot markets scored above a 110 index. These 18 markets yield 30% of total brand sales.

Avoid writing any recommendations in the situation analysis. *Phrase your SWOT so that it reports facts only - no goals, objectives or strategies.*

6. Timing & Purchase Cycle

Timing is everything in media. When should you advertise this brand? Some products are highly seasonal. If there is relatively consistent demand for your product throughout the year (or for a solid block of time such as 3 months or 6 months) a CONTINUOUS media schedule may be needed. If consumers do not purchase your product every month (e.g. appliances, cars, tires, etc.) a FLIGHTING schedule may be justifiable. PULSING may be a good strategy if demand is fairly continuous, but with heavier demand in key months. Study consumption of the brand and category. Know when sales are highest and lowest. Once the SWOT discovers key timing facts, extra weight (GRPs) can be used in the heaviest consumption periods. For example, if 60% of sales occur in July, this may call for 60% of the GRP weight in July, for one month *before* July.

- Is life cycle relevant? If this is a new product introduction, when should advertising launch?
- Seasonality - which months are most important?
- Should campaign launch before or during peak sales period?
- When does competition advertise most heavily? Should you have a strategy to deal with it? Match it? Exceed it?
- What is the purchase cycle for this product? If purchased often (more than once a month), frequent reminder advertising may be appropriate.
- Will purchase cycle influence the frequency strategy in a media plan?
- Are any specific days of the week important?
- Is there a time of day when most purchases are made? Which media could reach target closest to this time?
- What time of day is product consumed or used?
- Should media weight (GRP's) follow monthly sales?
- Any sales promotion events? Is media support needed? When? Why?
- Is a specific time of month important for this product?
- Any holidays that might influence consumption?
- Can weather or climate in geographic regions be used strategically?

7. Questions About The Media Mix

Although last on the list, this is one of the most critical issues in your plan. Media mix is the combination of media and vehicles that suit this brand best. The media mix should also address which environment is best for the brand. Kid's cereal, for example, would not be appropriate for late night TV. Technical products (computers, cars, etc.) may require long copy, and the higher credibility of the magazine environment. Guerilla marketing may work marketing XBox or Playstation to teenagers, but may not work as well for many adult products. High tech products may also require interactive Internet buys. Remember to state your observations about the brand and media options under consideration – and to write them as facts, not as goals. Do not make any media recommendations yet. Ask these questions:

- How much Internet or social media is appropriate for your brand?
- Which media/vehicles match the lifestyle of your target audience?
- Will budget allow you to match or outspend the competition using the same media mix as competitors?
- Are there any weaknesses in competitor's media mix?
- Do you have enough competitive media data to create a Share of Voice (SOV) analysis?
- Does your brand enjoy clear advantages over the competition? If so, consider meeting them head-on in their own media.
- Which media would work best for this brand? Why? Any marketing incentives for using social media? Radio? TV? Mobile Media? Internet? Magazines? Social? Guerilla media? Media mix is the

very heart of your media strategy. Sound research here is vital supported by solid rationales.

- Is purchase decision high or low involvement? If high involvement, can print media be effective?
- Is the message simple or complex?
- How, if at all, should the Internet be used for this brand?
- Is message heavy with information?
- How much time or space is needed to say it?
- Is creative concept flexible enough to work effectively across all media?
- Should product/service be demonstrated?
- Does product need to be shown visually? Why?
- Is color important in your media mix for this brand?
- Would print be effective? Would coupons induce trial? What possible cross promotions might work with other brands or categories?
- Are commuters likely to purchase? Where? When? Which media are best to reach them?
- Have you calculated effective frequency for your media mix? (If available, use Ostrow model). How many exposures are estimated to get response?

"Gotchas" That Destroy SWOT Credibility

Biggest offense: Inadequate research. Clients do not value opinions; they want valid information, and nothing improves validity more than evidence backed up by primary and secondary sources. Primary research generally refers to research contracted directly by the agency or client; secondary research comes from syndicated sources or published materials in the library or on the internet. Secondary sources are a good start, but don't stop there.

Using only secondary research suggests laziness. Clients expect you to tell them something they don't know. This could be accomplished with primary research. If time and money preclude a scientific study, conduct something as simple as a non-probability intercept survey in a mall, or sample a few people on the phone. A phone call to a store manager takes minimal effort, or even better, visit him/her in the store, and take photos on site, etc. For example, if you're assigned to work on the Harley Davidson business, visit the store and talk with the sales people. Hang out with customers and get inside the Harley culture. Provide evidence of all merchandising and promo strategies. If you're marketing a packaged goods product, visit the store section and map the number of shelf facings occupied by your brand and all competitors. (Facings = number of packages that "face" the customer horizontally on the shelf). How many shelves (vertically) does each brand occupy? Does your brand (or a competitive brand) capitalize on end cap displays? Talk to customers. Study them as they shop for brands in your category.

Failure to cite sources kills your credibility. If you don't cite sources, or bury your sources, credibility is weakened.

Poor organization discourages reading your plan. Avoid fluff and filling pages with opinions. Unsubstantiated thinking jumps off the page and suggests last minute effort.

Use subheads and avoid "fluff-heads" that say nothing. Write complete "headlines" and don't worry about length. Hook the reader by selling a concept with compelling suheads. Example: "Social Media Dominates Red Bull's Media Mix."

Lazy writing is a major "gotcha." Clients (and professors) can always tell when you're submitting a first draft.

Late work brands you, whatever the reason. Your reason for lateness automatically reveals a lot about you to the client. What's the best excuse for lateness? Not, "I was sick or my car broke down." Man up and tell the client, "No excuse - it won't happen again."

ORGANIZING A MEDIA PLAN

Anatomy of a Media Plan

This chapter illustrates all the parts of the plan in linear order with examples for each. The chapter "University Media Plan" provides excellent examples of well-crafted media objectives, rationales, and strategies. Important Note: There are as many models for writing media plans as there are ad agencies. The winning example follows many (but not all) of the conventions shown here. Unless your professor instructs you otherwise, follow the outline shown below – it covers the basics.

The media plan is comprised of five sections: Each section should start on a new page.

> **Model Media Plan:**
>   I. Executive Summary
>   II. SWOT-Situation Analysis
>   III. Creative Brief-Creative Strategy
>   IV. Media Objectives & Strategies
>   V. Appendix

I. Executive Summary

Typically one to two pages in length, this is a tight, definitive synopsis that reveals the highlights of your plan. It should highlight the strategic genius that drives your media plan, and after reading your summary, the marketing VP should know if the rest of the plan is worth reading.

II. SWOT - Situation Analysis Section (Start on a new page)

Recommended length: There is no absolute length for a situation analysis, but it typically runs 4-6 pages. Avoid prose style. Write in business/technical style using outline format. Use "call out" boxes and compelling subheads to draw the reader's attention to vital points.

A good way to approach the SWOT is to ask intelligent questions about your brand's marketing situation, and craft your answers into statements of relevant marketing/media facts that will drive your media objectives and strategies. (See SWOT – Situation Analysis in previous chapter.)

Remember, this is *not* a place for media objectives or strategies. *Avoid recommendations and rationales.* Instead, be descriptive and factual. A situation analysis reports the important facts and history relevant to the brand - *it never includes objectives or strategies about what you plan to do.*

Based on the **Marketing Checklist For Media Planners** that you studied in the previous chapter, your situation analysis or SWOT should include detailed information on the following:

- Analysis of Marketing Objectives & Strategies
- Competitive Considerations
- Creative History of the Brand
- Target Audience
- Geography Questions
- Timing & Purchase Cycle
- Questions about The Media Mix

III. Creative Brief – Creative Strategy (Start on a new page)

Along with marketing considerations, creative is equally important in driving the media plan. Media decisions must be integrated with the brand's creative strategy. Media objectives and strategies must be consistent with the creative strategy. For example, if your brand's success depends on a creative concept on facebook, this position must be clearly articulated in the brief. Some professors may require a few creative executions to accompany your brief. This can be useful in helping to integrate the media plan with the message.

Creative Brief

The Creative Brief is a one-page document defining the creative strategy. This brief includes five main points:

1. Communication Objective
State exactly what you expect the advertising to accomplish. Awareness? Trial purchase? Brand loyalty? Increase customer traffic in the retail store?

2. Creative Strategy – Brand Position
At the heart of any creative strategy, positioning describes *how you want your brand to be perceived by the consumer*. It describes your niche in the mind of the consumer. Begin by identifying your brand's existing position. For example, assume the brand is Harley Davidson's Sportster targeted primarily at thirty-something women. Harley-Davidson is an expert at inclusion marketing, and it's impossible to do inclusion marketing for the Sportster unless you understand the thirty-something female. Harley knows she wants to identify with the Harley brand – hence the Sportster is positioned as an entry-level bike with all the classic sound and power women expect from a Harley. HD understands that women want to be *included* in the Harley culture; they want to be *perceived* as legitimate Harley owners. The last thing they want is to be singled out as sissy bike owners.

3. Promise
What is the major *benefit* your product promises to the user? **Caution**: A product feature is not a benefit. For example, the Harley Sportster's 850 cc engine is a product feature. *The benefit* is power and a throaty Harley report.

4. Tone
What is the tone of voice of your advertising? Friendly? Serious? Light-hearted? Humorous? Thoughtful? Use one or two words to describe the tone.

5. Tag line

A tag line or slogan gives continuity to a campaign. Use economy of language, make it memorable, rhythmic, and make sure it reflects the advertising position.

For example:

Harley-Davidson
Live to Ride.
Ride To Live.®

IV. Media Objectives & Strategies (Start on a new page)

Media objectives and strategies are dual engines that drive the whole media plan. Considered the heart of any plan, you'll find *six basic media strategies and objectives* illustrated in depth in the next chapter. The six include:

- Target Audience & Media Mix
- Reach, Frequency & GRPs
- Scheduling & Timing
- Media Budget
- Geography
- Sales Promotion

V. Appendix

The appendix is a place for exhibits in the very back of the plan – and includes data that supports your plan but is too lengthy or complicated to include in the main section. One important rule of thumb: If it's really important, don't hide it in the appendix, because it is often quickly scanned or even ignored by the client.

THE ART OF WRITING MEDIA OBJECTIVES AND STRATEGIES

Kirkham Motor Sports Cobra

Tom Kirkham and his son, Dave, owners of Kirkham Motor Sports, use a bottom-up business model. They trekked the globe seeking out parts suppliers and tooling up a factory to authentically replicate the classic Ford Shelby Cobra. They succeeded in creating the most authentic hand crafted Cobra replica in the world, now so popular they always have a waiting list. Each Cobra is a one-off classic, true to the original in every detail from aircraft braided hoses to the buffed aluminum body. It's the world's last and only aluminum skinned Cobra still hand crafted in the tradition of the famous original.

The Cobra bodies are formed, hand-finished and buffed to a near polish by highly skilled craftsmen in Warsaw, Poland, and then shipped to the US. These craftsmen learned their trade building Soviet MIG

fighters in a factory now converted for Cobra production. Tongue in cheek, Dave Kirkham told one of his former MIG fighter craftsmen, "I want all the body parts to fit together with near zero tolerance - I want this car to hold water when it's finished." During his next visit to the factory, Dave found the trunk of a finished Cobra filled with water, and it didn't leak a drop. Each Cobra that roars out of the Kirkham shop has a tamper-proof nameplate and serial number. The Kirkhams were forced to brand their Cobras after critics complained they couldn't distinguish their $100,000 replicas from the original Shelby Cobras at car shows and auctions.

Think of Media Objectives/Strategies as Art

Just as Cobra Craftsmen are perfectionists, marketers and media planners must be devoted to communicating both the tangible and the psychological benefits of a brand. Similar to handcrafting a classic race car, crafting media objectives and strategies demands rigorous attention to detail, and a passion for strategic planning that builds brands into familiar icons. Not only must the media plan achieve a tight fit with marketing, indeed the entire media plan is a marketing document because media objectives and strategies are driven by exhaustive marketing research. *Media planners are charged with crafting objectives into measurable goals and fitting them seamlessly with strategies that build brand equity.*

Using product examples, the next few pages explain the process of how to write your own media objectives and strategies. Each case, while based on brand research, does take some liberties for the sake of illustration.

A full set of media objectives and strategies for Coca-Cola is provided at the end of this chapter. After studying the Coke Mini-Case, you may want to bookmark it for future reference. It offers a full set of media objectives and strategies - use them as models to help you learn the art of writing your own media plans.

Measurable Media Objectives

Measurability requires marketers to be accountable for both marketing and media goals. If the marketing objectives for the brand are clearly articulated, media objectives emerge naturally out of these goals. Driven by intelligent marketing objectives, measurable media objectives establish the direction for the brand's entire communications plan. A planner's success or failure rests on the research, imagination and passion invested into writing measurable media objectives.

Writing the Media Objective –Identifying the Goal

The secret to writing media objectives is to focus on the goal – define exactly what you want to do. Whether targeting buyers for Subway sandwiches or Biolage shampoo, first discover which media most effectively communicate with the target. Since you are almost always aiming at a moving target exposed to dozens of media, *triangulate your objective from multiple perspectives.* Connect with the target on many levels – from traditional media to product sampling to social media web sites. Conduct exhaustive consumer analysis – how can you persuade someone to act on your message unless you know her both demographically and psychographically? Target analysis ranges from digging through oceans of quantitative data to in-depth qualitative research on attitudes and lifestyles. Syndicated data and other secondary sources often do not go deep enough – that's when you begin doing your own primary research.

Writing the Media Strategy – How to Achieve the Goal

When Marshall McLuhan theorized, "the medium is the message," advertisers listened because they realized that *the medium is loaded with qualitative meaning independent of the ad copy.* For example, a commercial on *Rachel Ray* on TV engages the heart and mind very differently than does the same ad in *Everyday with Rachael Ray* magazine, or a tweet about Rachel's roasted peppers and balsamic chicken. Always craft your message to fit the medium – not the other way around. If you're an educated media planner, you no longer consider TV a no-brainer buy. You should buy media wherever the target audience is *involved*, not just where the GRPs are highest. How can I move her? Which magazines does she wait for each week? Is she on Facebook? Twitter? Which web sites does she bookmark? Which sports does she spend money on? How much time does she spend working out?

There is no "recipe" for writing objectives or strategies. Each must be custom designed based on the marketing ingredients that make up the brand. Nevertheless, there is no better way to learn how to write objectives/strategies than to study examples of successful brands. Here are some examples using the marriage of two famous brands, Apple and Nike.

Example of Marketing Objective: *Apple and Nike will team up in a cross promotion to boost demand by 10% for two existing products. Capitalizing on the synergy inherent in the personality of both brands, Nike+ SportWatch GPS and Apple iPhone will be integrated into a single product.*

The product resulting from this objective was the Nike+ SportWatch GPS plus iPhone that "helps the miles unfold and lets you hear real-time voice feedback on your run – all to your favorite music including the one song that always gets you through the home stretch."

Example of a Target Audience Objective: *The primary target audience for both brands is composed of age 18-24 college females. Combining their love of popular culture along with an obsession for running and fitness, the marriage of Apple iPhone and Nike+ SportWatch GPS is a match made in cross-promotion heaven.*

Example of Media Objective: *Because of our target's frequent consumption of popular culture such as iTunes, heavy usage of mobile media and social networking like Facebook and twitter, 40% of the budget will be focused on SEO (Search Engine Optimization) and social media with 60% dedicated to sales promotion and traditional media.*

Example of a Media Strategy: *Traditional and social media will be integrated to work seamlessly to complement each other throughout the campaign. Begin campaign with an April kickoff on MTV. Nike+ SportWatch GPS ads and graphics will be painted visually and musically on Facebook, Google, hulu, digg, and YouTube. Nike+ SportWatch GPS shoe signs will be posted in 500 gyms in the top 50 metro markets. Radio will be used in the top 50 markets following the TV kickoff.*

Notice how objectives tell you very specifically *what* is to be accomplished, while strategies tell you *how*.

How to Write Media Objectives & Strategies

Although only a partial media plan, this Coca-Cola mini case study that follows provides a complete model of the art of writing media objectives and strategies. Keep in mind that the objectives/strategy section is the most vital part of any media plan. This is where the client will spend the most time, and it's where you either win or lose the business.

No Objective is an Island. One of the most important concepts in this case is that all six objectives/strategies are interdependent. As you study the case, take note how all six of the objectives and strategies are interwoven. Interplay between them is not only expected, it's essential since each objective affects a neighboring objective, or a related objective up or down the line. Repetition of key points is normal in this section of the plan - most objectives/strategies are linked in some way with at least two or three others. The most thoughtful media plan recognizes this interdependence and justifies it by strategically linking all the parts together.

Brevity and Wit. Note the attention to detail in the Coke Case. Media plans demand measurable, actionable objectives that drive imaginative strategies. Also note the economy of words; media objectives are short and to the point. Although typically a bit longer, media strategies are never verbose; strategies should employ the same economy of words used in objectives.

Six Recommended Media Objectives/Strategies. There is no absolute number of media objectives/strategies for any media plan, but based on experience, we recommend the following set of six. Note that each of the six requires its own objective and strategy—twelve "points" altogether.

Media Objectives & Strategies

   I. Target Audience & Media Mix
   II. Reach, Frequency & GRPs
   III. Scheduling & Timing
   IV. Media Budget
   V. Geography
   VI. Sales Promotion

Six Media Objectives/Strategies for Coca-Cola

I. Target Audience and Media Mix Objective: Over thirty percent of Coke's North American soft drink volume is consumed by teens 13-18. The target audience goal for this campaign is to increase the Coke brand experience (consumption) by 20% among teens 13-18 by reaching a new teen market that doesn't think or drink like any other. This campaign will create a tangible brand experience reaching over 1 million teens in 10 DMA markets using radio/TV to announce a guerilla-marketing event, the "Free Coke & Burger Bash."

Remember: **A media strategy tells how to achieve the media objective**: Study how the following media strategy delivers the Coca-Cola objective stated above:

Target Audience and Media Mix Strategy: We will break away from prior media strategies; breaking away includes announcing the "Free Coke & Burger Bash" with YouTube video and Facebook product page. In addition, youth-focused cable TV and local FM radio will also be used. March 1st launches a teaser campaign on ESPN Sports Center, MTV Real World, MTV2, VH1, SITV, FUSE and the top 5 FM rock stations in each market. Teaser ads will build excitement leading up to the "Bash" on April 1. April begins a month-long guerilla campaign with thirty Coca-Cola "Can-Vans" rotating among the biggest middle schools and high schools in Coke's top ten DMA markets. Free Coca-Cola and burgers will be offered during lunch and after-school for 1-2 weeks on locations adjacent to local schools. Winning numbers for 100 prizes daily will be printed on Coke cans and announced on www.Coca-Cola.com. Visits to Coke's web site will offer free sports gear, free McDonald's and Wendy's grub, free Cinemark movie passes, and free iTunes music downloads.

II. Reach, Frequency and GRP Objective: Achieve 80% reach during the kick-off month (350 GRPs) with average 4.5 frequency. Reach will range from 70–85% over the life of the campaign. Frequency will bottom at 3.0. The non-traditional reach goal (event marketing) is to get 40% of teens in each school to visit the Coca-Cola "Can Vans" for a burger and a Coke. Hard counts will be taken each day in each location.

Reach, Frequency and GRP Strategy: Traditional media will peak during the kick-off with 350 GRPs in TV and FM radio. Media weight will go toward a teaser campaign on ESPN *Sports Center*, MTV *Real World*, MTV2. VH1 buys include *Rock Docs* and *Tough Love*. Syfy will run *Ghost Hunters*, *Eureka* and *Stargate Universe*. FUSE includes *On the Record* and *Hip Hop Shop*. The top 5 FM rock stations will run Burger Bash ads mornings and afternoons in each market.

*** *Did you notice the integration between objective/strategy 1 and 2? Integrated marketing demands all components of your plan be stitched together. If you want to make a living as a marketer, be willing to invest* *the time to write intelligently. It's virtually impossible to write a top notch plan on the first draft.*

III. Scheduling and Timing Objective: Campaign kick-off begins with a teaser campaign running throughout March to preempt the competition. Traditional media run continuously in March, April, and May. "Free Coke & Burger Bash" service begins April 1. The Coke Can-Van will open 1-2 hours during lunch periods and reopen two hours after school. The "Bash" runs 1-2 weeks in April and May.

Scheduling and Timing Strategy: Teaser campaign (350 GRPs) runs during the March launch to generate interest and awareness. The broadcast schedule in April/May drops to 300 and 250 GRPs respectively. Although reach/frequency will bottom at 70/3, this is adequate to sustain awareness. Broadcast buys in TV will not run until after school is out, between 4 pm and midnight. FM radio ads will run from noon through 12 pm daily to remind teens about the Coke & Burger event.

IV. Media Budget Objective: Coke's $4.5 million budget is limited to spending in 10 DMAs. Markets will receive a percentage of total budget based on their Estimated Value (EV%) rankings from a spreadsheet analysis of all 10 markets.

Media Budget Strategy: An analysis was conducted on the 10 DMAs based on these criteria:

- Total teens (boys and girls) ages 13-18 in each market
- Soft drink category sales by market
- Coca-Cola sales by market

The $4.5 million budget is allocated as follows:

- $3,000,000 in mass media (Cable TV, FM radio, Internet buys) in 10 DMAs.
- $1,000,000 for Coke & burger products plus leasing/outfitting thirty Coke Can-Vans.
- $500,000 covers 100 prizes daily: Free sports gear, free McDonald's and Wendy's grub, free Cinemark movie passes, and free iTunes music downloads.

V. Geography Objective: Ten middle and high school markets are targeted for the "Free Coke & Burger Bash" guerilla-marketing event. All cable TV and FM radio buys are restricted to spot buys in these 10 markets. This will be a spot-only media buy.

Geography Strategy: MRI and CMR data combined with Coca-Cola's proprietary marketing database provided information for a spreadsheet evaluation of the top 40 DMAs. Market selections are predicated on EV% growth potential for Coke products. In ranking order, the 10 metros selected from the top 40 include:

Los Angeles	Houston
Chicago	Seattle-Tacoma
Atlanta	Miami
Philadelphia	Phoenix
San Francisco	Sacramento

Note: Be sure to generate a weighted spreadsheet (see exercise section of book) and include it with your SWOT. If multiple markets are being considered, **always include the spreadsheet analysis and results with your geography objective**.

The Coca-Cola spreadsheet analysis for this plan is based on four criteria:

- Total target males/females age 13-18 by market (DMA)
- Fast food sales volume by market (DMA)
- Canned soft drink sales volume by market (DMA)
- Annual discretionary spending by market (DMA)

VI. Sales Promotion Objective: Sales promotion carries the biggest responsibility in this campaign. Our goal is to increase the Coke brand experience by 20% among teens, and this increase will be accomplished through a guerilla-marketing event – the "Free Coke & Burger Bash." Internet goal: Generate 1 million visits (click-throughs) to Coca-Cola.com with 40% target penetration in all ten markets.

Sales Promotion Strategy: The "Free Coke & Burger Bash" is the primary vehicle for achieving the goal of increasing brand experience by 20% among teens. (20% increase = average 20% increased Coca-Cola consumption among teens compared to current Coke brand consumption in the 10 DMAs.) To achieve this goal, at least 40% of teens in the 10 DMAs must participate in a tangible brand experience during the "Bash" event. A tangible brand experience = one or more visits to the "Coke & Burger Bash." Thirty Coke "Can-Vans" will rotate (bi-weekly) among the highest enrollment middle schools and high schools in the top ten DMAs. Teaser ads (350 GRPs) announcing the "Bash" will run in March in teen dominated media. Ads will continue through April and May to stimulate traffic and induce trial. Fifteen second ads announcing "Free Coke & Burger Bash" will run on spot cable channels in all 10 markets.

The "Coke & Burger Bash" will open during lunch periods and after-school and last for 1-2 weeks on locations adjacent to each metro school. Number codes for 100 daily prizes will be printed on Coke cans and winners will be announced on www.Coca-Cola.com. Visits to Coke's web site will achieve 20% penetration among the target audience by offering additional chances at prizes—free sports gear, free McDonald's and Wendy's grub, free Cinemark movie passes, and free iTunes music downloads.

Companion Internet Strategy: Teen visits to the Coca-Cola web site will generate a permission-marketing database. Teens who give permission to receive email (Coke SURPRIZES) and tweets will increase brand loyalty by responding to additional Coca-Cola purchase incentives over a one-year internet marketing campaign.

Summary: Note the attention to detail, and the clear articulation of specific, measurable goals - the integration of relationship marketing, social media, sales promotion and mass media. Also note the imaginative use of targeted promotions and careful attention to media mix strategy and targeted vehicles. Everything is stitched together to ensure that every objective and strategy pushes and pulls together.

Team up with a Diet Coke to save calories!

ABC's OF WITTY, INTELLIGENT WRITING

Why Does This Executive Hate Reading Plans?

Trey Hall, entrepreneur and President of Consumer Concept Group said:

> *"I hate reading plans. I don't know a single executive who enjoys it. I do it because I can't spend a dime until your plan is rock solid with intelligent writing. I really hate it when writers fill it with fluff. You know when your plan contains genius. It's also obvious when your plan is filled with helium. It looks and feels like a last-minute, desperate attempt to fill paper. If you can't hold my attention with witty, intelligent writing, you'll be sorting my mail tomorrow."*

Make Good Writing a Passion

Good business writing skills are in top demand whether you end up working as a brand manager, media planner, sales rep, account manager, creative director, or most any other career. Make writing your passion. Without strong writing skills it's unlikely you'll get hired into management positions. Even if you do get hired in a top corporation, you won't go far unless you can write. Virtually every important business decision is driven by words, whether on paper or electronically. Invest whatever time it takes to write intelligent, organized media plans.

Quality Writing Can Sell or Kill Your Plan

Tweaking GRPs and dollars gives you a false sense of security when you should be spending more time writing. Fine tuning GRPs is great if you have time, but the written plan is more important than pushing reach or frequency a few points higher. A rule of thumb is to budget one fourth of your time for number crunching, and put the remaining three fourths into strategic planning, writing and editing. A brilliant media strategy is totally wasted unless it is communicated with brilliance. Your client has to "get it."

Kevin Killion, former Media Research Director for DDB Needham Worldwide, Chicago, wrote the memo shown below. Motivated by an intern's "particularly awkward report," he wrote these pointers for new planners and researchers (used by permission). His attitude about written work resonates with many corporate executives.

Memo To: Future interns
From: Kevin Killion
             Media Research Director, DDB Needham Worldwide

Subject: **Guidelines For Writing Plans**

Keep It Interesting
No one has to read your business paper (unlike a term paper). Therefore, you must make your paper useful, and, more than that, interesting. An "inverted pyramid" newspaper style works well: give intriguing facts or observations first, and follow with the details.

Outline
Always start the project with a rough outline of your proposed topics. This helps you to cover all the areas you intend. It also helps you to keep your project well organized.

Organization
The paper should be organized clearly into bite-sized sections. Each section (a few paragraphs) should be set off with a header. For any paper of more than a few pages, organize related topics into chapters. Papers of ten or more pages should start with an inviting introduction page, followed by an "executive summary." This helps the readers to glean your key points even if they don't read the whole paper. It also helps them decide if they can benefit by reading further.

Clear organization of your paper has these benefits:

- It keeps your thoughts coherent.
- It lets readers find selected sections easily.
- It builds a better case by flowing logically.
- It looks less makeshift and more professional.

Accuracy
Our lawyers peruse every word written by the copywriters. You should be no less scrupulous. Here are some common problems:

- **Generalization**: "Viewers today prefer the variety on cable." Well, some do, perhaps even many or most, but not all as this sentence suggests. Be specific; what percent of viewers?
- **Unfounded Suppositions**: In many cases, you may not be able to prove a claim with existing data. However, even if the claim seems self-evident, you should qualify any such premise with such words as "perhaps," "we suspect that" or "many researchers believe that." Your arguments must also be *logically* accurate. Conclusions should follow from stated premises. Moreover, you should learn to develop your skills in identifying logic problems in materials you read.

Text and Tables
Some people like pure text. Other people love charts and tables. Make your paper acceptable to both. Give tables when appropriate, showing base numbers, percentages or indexes in detail. A preceding paragraph should take the key or most interesting information from the table and spell it out for the reader in English sentences, preferably with some interpretation.

You should always avoid statements like "Here is a chart of ratings by daypart." This requires readers to analyze the table themselves. It sounds like you are saying "Here's a table. I can't figure it out - - you give it a try!"

Similarly, avoid juicy sentences based on charts which you are not including. This invites readers to either beg for details, or to lose interest in the paper altogether.

Courtesies
It is guaranteed that there will be deletions, additions and revisions. Leave room for notes that will be made on your draft.

If your plan will be edited into final draft by an assistant, it is unlikely he/she will be able to interpret your abbreviations. If you want to say "households," say that, not "HH." Tables should be "assistant-ready" in the form you want them to appear.

Dos and Don'ts for Writing Your Media Plan

Do:
1. Outline all of your objectives and strategies before using Media Flight Plan.
2. Organize your plan into bite-sized sections.
3. Include an executive summary.
4. Use subheads liberally - give them substance so they seduce the reader into the text.
5. Use white space liberally.
6. Leave room for notes with wide margins.
7. Take pity on the reader - keep it interesting or lose me.
8. Number the pages.
9. Avoid generalizations; be specific. Back your work up with hard numbers when possible.
10. Edit, edit, edit for accuracy and clarity.
11. Reduce graphs/charts to smallest size possible and integrate them into the text.
12. Explain tables in English sentences.
13. Label pie charts with words, not legends.
14. Write to the client - use third person.
15. Keep a spare computer ink cartridge in reserve. (Few computer supply stores are open at 1 am).
16. Impress client with primary & secondary research. Cite sources so client can't miss them.
17. Check spelling and grammar. Remember, you're selling yourself as a communicator.
18. Edit the fluff - it's painfully obvious when people fill pages with helium. The corollary: use active voice, not passive. It is direct and requires fewer words.
19. Start early - submit work on time.
20. Expect your computer to crash - make frequent back-ups.
21. Expect print-out problems at the last minute.
22. Allow time to edit, rewrite, and print final drafts.
23. Expect malaria the night before deadline.

Don't:
1. Don't use superlatives like "low cost" or "high reach."
2. Don't write long paragraphs, and don't cram too much on a page. Use white space.
3. Don't expect the client to believe you without adequate backup. Cite secondary and primary sources, not opinion.

4. Don't fill pages to "get the assignment done." Your work will torture the reader if your writing lacks passion, because it will advertise that you threw the stuff together in one day.

5. Seduce the reader with witty headlines and intelligent thinking.

6. Don't isolate huge charts/graphs on single pages. It looks tacky.

7. Appendix is the appendix. Don't bury things the client NEEDS TO KNOW in the back of your plan.

8. Never require the client to perform hard labor to understand your graphics. For example, label pie charts in plain English - never use legends that require translation.

9. Don't throw in tables or graphs without explanation. That says, "Here, you figure it out."

10. Don't forget to number the pages. Attention to detail is assumed by the client.

11. Don't pop a staple in the corner. If you're trying to look professional, bind it.

12. Don't blame computer crashes on anybody but yourself. Saving backups is your responsibility.

13. Don't expect client to gush with sympathy when you're late for most any reason. If you're late, don't make excuses - it reveals too much about you. The best excuse is: "I have no excuse."

14. Don't make last minute excuses. Inform client one or two days ahead if a delay is imminent.

TOOLS FOR WRITING MEDIA PLANS

Ostrow Model: Theoretical Model for Estimating Effective Frequency

The best (really the only) way to determine an appropriate effective frequency level is research. However, many clients either don't have funds or choose not to put resources into doing the necessary research. Nonetheless, clients often expect some idea of what it will take to break through. Many agencies use some form of model or checklist to estimate an appropriate level. Ostrow's approach provides a valuable theoretical base for novice planners by asking you to think about various aspects of your brand situation. It considers a combination of three strategic factors essential for estimating frequency: *Marketing, Copy, and Media.*

Ostrow's model *assumes that 3.0 as a benchmark* or starting point for estimating frequency. To apply this Model, *begin with this 3.0 benchmark*, and add or subtract from it based on the sum of the three parts.

Begin on the accompanying page by "testing" Glacier – use the questions posed in each of the three sub-headings in the model. Since 'Glacier' is a new brand, it gets the maximum +0.2 for *Established brand?* under the heading: **Marketing Factors That Affect Frequency**. Positive values increase frequency, while negative values obviously reduce it. Below is a convenient format for reporting your results:

Note: Ostrow Model is important for case studies—use this format to report results.

OSTROW MODEL EXAMPLE: Glacier Spring Water

Part I: Marketing Factors That Affect Frequency

Established brand? (No, it is a new national brand)	+.2
High market share? (No, Spot markets high, but not nationally)	+.1
Dominant brand? (Yes, in spot markets, but not nationally)	+.1
High brand loyalty? (Yes, in spot markets, but not nationally)	+.1
Long purchase cycle? (No, Short cycle—loyal users buy 2-4 six packs/month)	+.2
Product used occasionally? (No, Product consumed 3-5 times/week)	+.1
Need to beat competition? (Yes, Intense threat from competitors)	+.2
Advertising to older consumers/children? (Yes, Both included)	+.2
	+1.2

Part II: Copy Factors That Affect Frequency

Simple copy? (Yes, Message will be very simple)	-.2
Copy more unique than competition? (Yes, Better every campaign)	-.1
Continuing campaign? (No, this is a brand new creative concept)	+.2
Product sell copy? (Yes, Combination of image and product sell)	+.1
Single kind of message? (Yes, High continuity creative strategy)	-.2
To avoid wear out: new messages? (Yes, Copy strategy fresh, new)	-.2
Larger ad units? (No, Medium ad units; 15 sec. TV/30 sec. Radio)	-.1
	-.5

Part III: Media Factors That Affect Frequency

Lower ad clutter? (No, Media selected have high clutter)	+.2
Compatible editorial? (No, Limited opportunity for related editorial)	+.1
Attentiveness high? (No, Low involvement product category)	+.1
Continuous advertising? (No, Limited budget requires flighting)	+.1
Few media used? (No, Moderate media mix)	+.1
Opportunities for media repetition? (Yes, Strong media repetition)	-.2
	+.4

Calculating Freq. Estimate

1. Sum the totals for each of the parts to get three subtotals. See column of numbers on left, with subtotals.

2. Sum the results from the three subtotals. See below:

Summing Results
  +1.2
  - .5
  + .4
  +1.1 + 3.0 Benchmark = 4.1

4.1 is the estimated frequency for Glacier's media plan. The 4.1 estimate is based on strategic consideration of the 3 part model on next page.

Ostrow Model

Once you complete your model, use format on the previous page as a convenient way to report it.

Marketing Factors That Affect Frequency

Established brands	-.2	-.1	+.1	+.2	New brands
High market share	-.2	-.1	+.1	+.2	Low market share
Dominant brand in market	-.2	-.1	+.1	+.2	Smaller, less known brand
High brand loyalty	-.2	-.1	+.1	+.2	Low brand loyalty
Long purchase cycle	-.2	-.1	+.1	+.2	Short purchase cycle, high volume
Product used occasionally	-.2	-.1	+.1	+.2	Product used daily
			+.1	+.2	Need to beat competition
			+.1	+.2	Adv. to older consumers/children

Copy Factors That Affect Frequency

Simple copy	-.2	-.1	+.1	+.2	Complex copy
Copy more unique than competition	-.2	-.1	+.1	+.2	Copy less unique than competition
Continuing [old] campaign	-.2	-.1	+.1	+.2	New copy campaign
Product sell copy	-.2	-.1	+.1	+.2	Image type copy
Single kind of message	-.2	-.1	+.1	+.2	More difficult kinds of messages
To avoid wear out: new messages	-.2	-.1	+.1	+.2	Older messages
Larger ad units	-.2	-.1	+.1	+.2	Small ad units

Media Factors That Affect Frequency

Lower ad clutter in media mix	-.2	-.1	+.1	+.2	Higher ad clutter in media mix
Compatible editorial environment	-.2	-.1	+.1	+.2	Non-compatible environment
Attentiveness (to media) high	-.2	-.1	+.1	+.2	Attentiveness (to media) low
Continuous schedule campaign	-.2	-.1	+.1	+.2	Pulsed or flighted campaign
Few media used in media mix	-.2	-.1	+.1	+.2	Many media used
Opportunities for media repetition	-.2	-.1	+.1	+.2	Fewer opportunities

Source: Ostrow, Joseph W. by personal permission. First published in "Setting Frequency Levels," in Effective Frequency: The State of the Art. Copyright 1982. Note: Model edited by permission for Media Flight Plan.

Reach & Frequency Guidelines

Planners need to ask why on every decision, and provide answers for the client. Two of the most challenging questions in writing media objectives are: How much reach is enough? And, how much frequency is enough? These questions are also related to **Media Strategy**. Media objectives tell *what* the plan will accomplish - e.g., how much reach/frequency is needed? What percent of budget will be spent on TV? Media strategies tell *how* they will be accomplished - that is, which media can best accomplish the reach/frequency goals? Which vehicles? When is the best time to advertise? Is flighting called for? Which markets make sense? etc.

Review of Key Issues is Important. The "Ostrow Model" will help you to estimate frequency levels for your plan. Also review the MFP chapter titled "Organizing a Media Plan" for other important items to include in your plan.

Reach & Frequency Dilemma. As GRPs increase, both reach and frequency increase. But reach follows a law of diminishing returns--it is a curve that flattens as weight increases. Initially reach climbs fastest, then frequency takes over and begins to climb more quickly as reach grows ever more slowly. Most marketing situations force the planner to optimize one over the other. Two exhibits shown below are intended to help you deal with the reach/frequency dilemma. These exhibits are simple rules of thumb--most of these rules have exceptions based on the product and marketing situation at hand. Consider these exhibits starting points you can build on to extend your knowledge and experience with reach and frequency.

High vs. Low Reach/Frequency

Highest Reach - 99%

Most computer-based reach curves set 96-99% as the upper limit for reach. In theory, it is impossible to expose 100 percent of a population to any media plan. Some prospects will always be missed either by chance, or because of lifestyle differences. Remember, *Media Flight Plan* was created to play "what if." Experiment to see how high you can build reach while maintaining frequency at acceptable levels, and all inside a given budget.

Moderate Reach - 70 to 75%

Reaching three-fourths of your prospects is considered a respectable goal. Although it is usually desirable to reach as many prospects as possible, the trade-off between reach and frequency may force you to settle for moderate reach.

Lowest Reach - 50 to 60%

The authors suggest that reach not drop much lower than 50% of the target audience. The logic is that if a brand requires advertising, it will probably encounter some level of competition in the market. If the brand is to achieve reasonable exposure, 50% reach may be the minimum for survival. If budget forces your reach to drop below 50%, you may want to employ a flighting strategy to maintain reach levels.

Highest Average Frequency - 12

Most media researchers accept the notion that frequency can hit a point of diminishing returns. This is commonly called the "wearout" . Many studies have been conducted on wear out, which typically occurs somewhere between 6 and 12 exposures per month. Many variables, especially the quality of your creative affect when wearout actually occurs. Since few budgets can support continuous high frequency levels, this may be a moot issue for your brand.

Lowest Average Frequency - 2 to 3

Frequency can drop quite low and still be effective. John Phillip Jones (father of 'recency theory') theorizes that great creative executions have the ability to generate significant response after the first exposure. It is almost a maxim in many media circles, however, that the benchmark frequency for a media plan is three exposures/month. When the average frequency is three, most of the prospects reached are *exposed less than three times* (a small portion of the population, say a fifth, are couch potatoes who are exposed much more heavily than the rest of the population) .

Strategy Decision: Optimize Reach or Frequency?

Use the following guide to think about optimizing reach or frequency. The decision about which to optimize is *primarily a strategic decision based on in-depth intelligence about the marketing situation*. It is not always an either/or decision based on these questions alone. Know your brand, its market, the creative/sales promotion strategy, and the competition. Also, consider all media objectives and how they interact with each other, and how all strategic decisions work together in the plan.

Reach/Frequency Decision Model

The following lists are guidelines--not absolutes. They suggest situations where reach or frequency might be optimized, however, always let the brand objectives guide your decision--they carry far more weight than these general suggestions.

Optimize Reach

Product introduction
In growth phase of life cycle
Few competitors
Strong established brand
Brand leader in category
Brand awareness is higher
Higher market share
High involvement purchase decision
High interest in category
Often higher priced goods and services
Low to moderate competition in category
Infrequent purchase-once a month or less
Continuous advertising schedule
Powerful creative that stands out
Ad message easily understood
Expanding into new markets
Major sales promotion launch
Seasonal peak for sales

Optimize Frequency

Product introduction
Mature well known brand
Many competitors
Less established brand
Among bottom of category
Brand awareness is lower
Lower market share
Low involvement purchase decision
Low interest category
Often lower priced goods and services
Strong to intense competition in category
Frequent purchase-2+ times per month
Flighted schedule
Creative on par with other ads
Complex ad message
Status quo geographically
Moderate to low sales promo activity
Beginning new season for brand

Guidelines for Buys with Media Flight Plan

These minimum guidelines will help you make more realistic buys when using *MFP* software. Although ratings shown are for *Adults*, they can be considered rough minimums for any target audience when using MFP. It is recommended that you use or exceed the **Minimum Buy** for a daypart where indicated, and when using multiple dayparts in national television for example, that you meet the Minimum Monthly Buy. These guidelines should not be ignored, however, you may have a need to do something different based on your objectives and strategies. The minimums below are typical 'bare minimums'; you will probably be at somewhat higher levels.

Medium	Minimum Buy	Minimum Monthly Buy
Network Television Avg Rtg: 2.0-5.0 varies by daypart	20 GRPs in a single daypart = about 4 to 10 spots	If used, a minimum of 35-50 GRPs total should be planned across all forms/dayparts of national television, with a minimum of 15 GRPs in any single daypart/form.
Cable Television Avg Rtg: 0.1-2.0 varies by network	20 GRPs in a single daypart = about 10 to 200 spots	
Syndication Avg Rtg: 2.0	20 GRPs in a single daypart = about 10 spots	
Network Radio Avg Rtg: 0.5-2.0 varies by daypart	20 GRPs in a single daypart = about 10-40 spots	If used, 35-50 GRPs total across all dayparts
Internet/Digital Media Avg Rtg: doesn't apply	20 GRPs across all forms	20 GRPs across all forms

Medium	Minimum Buy	Minimum Monthly Buy
Magazines Avg Rtg: 5.0-12 varies by type	20-25 GRPs = about 2-3 insertions	If used, buy magazines in more than one month—avoid "one time Charlies"—one insertion per magazine over the plan
National Newspapers (USA Today, WSJ, etc) Avg Rtg: 2.0	10-20 GRPs = 5-10 insertions	10 GRPs if run with magazines (national newspapers are often treated as magazines, and can be included in the magazine total) 20 GRPs if alone
Spot Television Avg Rtg: 1.0-6.0 varies by daypart	20 GRPs per daypart = about 5-10 spots	If used, 35-50 GRPs total across all dayparts
Spot Cable Avg Rtg: 0.2	20 GRPs = about 100 spots	If used, 20 GRPs
Spot Radio Avg Rtg: 2.0-3.0	20 GRPs in a single daypart = about 10 spots	If used, 35-50 GRPs total across all dayparts
Local Newspaper-40% coverage* (equivalent to enough papers to equal roughly a 40 rating)	2 insertions = about 80 GRPs	Your ad would appear 2 times in the month for an ongoing campaign. For a "sale" 1 insert may be sufficient.
Outdoor*	25 Showing—this is the rough equivalent of 25 GRPs per day	25 showing
Direct Mail*	10 GRPs	10 GRPs

*Local Newspapers. In MFP, newspapers are one of the exceptions to buying with GRPs because of complications that come from keeping track of newspapers across 210 markets. To simplify purchasing spot newspapers, MFP assumes you will buy all the papers required to cover 40 percent of the market. Sometimes this would mean buying local weekly papers in addition to major papers in the market. When you buy one insertion in MFP, it means putting one insertion in each of the papers required to meet the 40 percent coverage level.

*Outdoor. In MFP there are three options for buying outdoor: 25, 50 or 100 showing. Each showing level equates to roughly that number of GRPs per day based on vehicle traffic for the month. In other words, a 25 showing would be estimated to produce 25 GRPs x 30 days = 750 GRPs. The high level of duplication (most boards are stationary, people's travel patterns are repetitive) results in high levels of frequency. More discussion about the characteristics of outdoor can be found in the MFP Tutorial.

* Direct Mail. A traditional reach curve doesn't work for direct mail. This is the only medium where one GRP could equal one percent reach among the audience, or that 25 GRPs could equal 25% reach. Theoretically, if you could afford it, 100 GRPs could deliver 100% reach. In reality, it's not that perfect—no direct mail list is completely accurate because of deaths, address changes, name changes, etc. or because people have intentionally omitted information or provided innaccurate information. One major drawback of direct mail is that it probably has the highest cost on a CPM basis when all the production, postage and other mailing costs are counted. Although exceptions do occur, it is rare for direct mail to be used in a national campaign due to prohibitive cost. For this reason, direct mail is only available as a spot option in MFP.

MEDIA MODELS

Many mathematical distributions are used in modeling various aspects of media and marketing. Some frequently used distributions are negative binomial, Poisson, and beta-binomial (BBD) which is used heavily in Media Flight Plan. It looks rather intimidating:

$$f\left(k\mid n,a,b\right)=\binom{n}{k}\frac{1}{\beta(a,b)}\int_{0}^{1}p^{k+a-1}(1-p)^{n-k+b-1}\,dp$$

Fortunately, we don't need to know how the 'guts' work to use BBD. Like going on a road trip, if we have a basic understanding of acceleration, the rules of the road, a key and a vehicle, we'll get to our destination. This chapter is intended to be like that—it'll give you a little background and send you on your way. We'll do some basic examples that will help you understand what's happening, but you can do the exercises here with the basic math you already know and a little help from a spreadsheet like Microsoft Excel. When you're done, you'll have a general idea of how BBD works, and how it came to be. (NOTE to math folks: we have taken some liberties herein—this is a 'conversational' explanation, not a formal treatise. Don't get your knickers in a twist).

Why is beta-binomial a popular model distribution? The simple answer is that it works! This distribution is very flexible, and can take on a wide variety of shapes, from 'u' shaped, to 'bell curvish', which allows it to be used to model different media whose reach accumulation follows different patterns. It has some other properties that make it attractive—it is generally possible to define an acceptable curve that covers the entire distribution from just two points, so it is simple. BBD is robust—it will never give you an impossible answer for reach—the answer always falls between zero and 100 percent (technically between 0 and 1.0). And unlike early models you probably haven't heard of (Agostini and Metheringham are two), it's well behaved. One well-known problem with Metheringham is that of occasional 'declining reach'—sometimes fairly high levels of weight produce a *lower(!)* reach than for lower weight levels—something that doesn't make sense in the real world. Nonetheless, Agostini and Metheringham's models pioneered the way for the development of models that are in use today. BBD isn't always the 'best' distribution, but it is almost always a reasonable one.

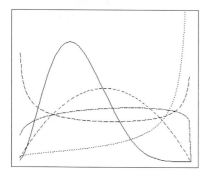
Beta Density for different levels of α and β

Basic probability: a building block. BBD follows from probability theory. Don't be alarmed—four simple common-sense concepts are sufficient for our needs. In fact, if you survived high school statistics, you already know them!

Independence means that the outcome of any test or trial doesn't affect the others. If you roll a die, getting a '3' on one roll does not affect the outcome of the next. In media, independence is not strictly true. For example, if a person reads one issue of *People* magazine, he or she may be more likely to read the next. However, with models, we typically don't focus on an individual. Over a group, media exposure often behaves nearly as if it were independent, even though a specific person's media habits may not be. For our purposes, we'll assume independence holds true.

And means that all desired events must occur, as in 'what is the probability that a viewer will read both issue one *and* issue two of *People?*' Without worrying about how we would measure the average issue, let's assume that *People* magazine has a rating of 15.0, which means that about fifteen percent of the population read a typical issue. The probability that two selected issues are read is the product of the individual probabilities—we just multiply them together, like this:

$$\textbf{E\#1]}\ (p_1 * p_2)$$
Example: 0.15 x 0.15 = .0225 (or about 2.3%)

So while 15.0 percent read a typical issue, only about 2.3 percent are expected to read both issues.

Or is the chance that *any* of a group of events would occur in a single trial, such as getting a 1 or a 5 on a single roll of a die. We calculate this by adding the individual probabilities, in this case 1/6 = 1/6 = 1/3. So what is the probability of reading issue one or issue two of *People* in a schedule? Each issue has a probability of 15%, but there is a problem with just adding the probabilities as we did for the single roll of the die:

$$\textbf{E\#2]}\ (p_1 + p_2)$$
Example: 15% + 15% = 30%

Any individual could read *both* issue one and issue two. When counting the readers of either issue one or issue two, it is incorrect to count readers of both issues twice. To remove the double-count, estimate readers of both using 'and,' then subtract that proportion from the sum of the probabilities. The true estimate of reading either issue is calculated this way, subtracting out the duplication:

$$\textbf{E\#3]}\ (p_1 + p_2) - (p_1 * p_2)$$
Example: (0.15+0.15)-(0.15*0.15) = 0.30 - .0225= .2775 or about 27.8%

Note it is usually more convenient to work probability problems if percentages are converted to decimals first as done in this example.

Not is the likelihood an event does not occur, such as 'not reading the third issue of *People*.' It can easily be calculated by subtracting the probability of an event from 1 (e.g. the sum of the probabilities of an event happening and not happening must equal 1.0 — or 100%). The probability of not seeing the specific issue three (or any other specific issue) is:

$$\textbf{E\#4]}\ (1-p)$$
Example: 1.0 - 0.15 = 0.85 or 85%

With this small statistical 'toolbox,' these operations can be strung together to estimate the reach of various combinations of issues. How about 'read the first or second issue, and not the third?'

'first or second'　　'and'　'not third'

[(0.15 +0.15)-(0.15 x 0.15)]　x　(1.0 - 0.15) = 0.2775 x 0.85 = 0.2358, or about 23.6%

Putting a schedule together. Using the concepts of 'independence', 'and', 'not' and 'or', it is possible to estimate readership of a schedule in *People* using just the average rating and basic probability. With these tools, you can estimate total reach, average frequency and GRPs, as well as estimate what proportion of the audience will read any given number of issues.

Let's think through the process using a specific example of 4 issues of *People*. Reading zero issues means 'not read issue 1 *and* not read issue 2 *and* not read issue 3 *and* not read issue 4'. By multiplying the 'not average rating' for each issue together, the result is the proportion 'not reading any.'

For reading exactly 1 issue in a schedule of 4, sum up the probabilities of all the ways to see only one issue: issue 1 and not issue 2, 3 and 4; issue 2 and not issue 1, 3 and 4; and so forth. The first way to see 'only one issue' using probability rules would be 0.15 * 0.85 *0.85 * 0.85 = 0.092 or 9.2 percent for 'read only the first issue and none of the others.' Thinking about this for a moment, it becomes obvious that which issue is read and which are not is irrelevant. The result will always be multiplying the same probabilities, just in a different sequence. The result is the same each time. It doesn't really matter which way only one issue is seen, just that it occurs exactly once. As a shortcut, multiplication could be used instead of summing the result four times. Four ways to read only one issue times 9.2% gives an estimate of 36.8%.

For the twos and threes, a similar process is used to add up all the possible ways to see two or three issues and multiply the probability of seeing two or three by the number of ways it could occur.

For 'saw exactly four', there is only one way: 'read issue 1 *and* read issue 2 *and* read issue 3 *and* read issue 4.' To get the estimate, simply multiply that value average rating times itself 4 times to get the estimated proportion reading all four issues.

This is the process used to estimate the frequency distribution of a magazine schedule using probability. Estimating a frequency distribution is as simple as figuring out the probability of seeing a certain number of issues and multiplying that by the number of ways it could happen. 'The number of ways it could happen' in conjunction with the probability is called the 'binomial expansion.' You may recognize 'the number of ways' as the method used to figure combinations of things, for example, 'how many ways can four issues be read 2 at a time'. The mathematical shorthand for combinations is $\binom{n}{k}$. Related to the example, the number on the top ('n') is the total number of issues; the one on the bottom ('k') is how many are read. In the introduction to this chapter, this notation appears at the beginning of Beta Binomial function. It is calculated like this:

$$\text{E\#5]} \quad \frac{k!}{n!(k-n)!}.$$

'!' is short for 'factorial' and is defined as multiplying the factorial term by all the integers less than it (except for 0). 4! equals 4*3*2*1, or 24. By definition, 0! is 1 (i.e. there is only one way to take nothing). In the four issue example of *People*, the full expansion of 0,1,2,3 or 4 issues can be calculated:

# Issues	Combinatorial Formula	Result: Number of Ways
0 of 4	$\binom{0}{4} = \frac{4!}{0!(4-0)!} = \frac{4*3*2*1}{1*(4*3*2*1)} = \frac{24}{24}$	1 way to see exactly 0 issues
1 of 4	$\binom{1}{4} = \frac{4!}{1!(4-1)!} = \frac{4*3*2*1}{1*(3*2*1)} = \frac{24}{6}$	4 ways to see exactly 1 issue
2 of 4	$\binom{2}{4} = \frac{4!}{2!(4-2)!} = \frac{4*3*2*1}{2*1*(2*1)} = \frac{24}{4}$	6 ways to see exactly 2 issues

# Issues	Combinatorial Formula	Result: Number of Ways
3 of 4	$\binom{3}{4} = \dfrac{4!}{3!(4-3)!} = \dfrac{4*3*2*1}{3*2*1*(1)} = \dfrac{24}{6}$	4 ways to see exactly 3 issues
4 of 4	$\binom{4}{4} = \dfrac{4!}{4!(4-4)!} = \dfrac{4*3*2*1}{4*3*2*1*(1)} = \dfrac{24}{24}$	1 way to see exactly 4 issues

Now that all the ways one could be exposed to 0,1,2,3 or 4 issues are calculated, the probability of each level of exposure can be estimated using probability rules. Continuing with *People* magazine, with an average issue rating of 15.0:

Probability of reading	Formula	Result (rounded)
0 of 4	*Ex: not see #1 and not see#2 and not see #3 and not see #4* =(1.0-0.15) * (1.0-0.15)* (1.0-0.15)* (1.0-0.15) =0.85*0.85*0.85*0.85 **or alternatively $0.15^0 * 0.85^4$**	0.5220 or 52.20%
1 of 4	*Ex: see #1 and not see#2 and not see #3 and not see #4* =0.15 * (1.0-0.15)* (1.0-0.15)* (1.0-0.15) =0.15 *0.85*0.85*0.85 **or alternatively $0.15^1 * 0.85^3$**	0.0921 or 9.21%
2 of 4	*Ex: see #1 and see#2 and not see #3 and not see #4* =0.15 * 0.15 * (1.0-0.15)* (1.0-0.15) =0.15 *0.15*0.85*0.85 **or alternatively $0.15^2 * 0.85^2$**	0.0163 or 1.63%
3 of 4	*Ex: see #1 and see#2 and see #3 and not see #4* =0.15 *0 .15 *0 .15 * (1.0-0.15) =0.15 *0.15*0.15*0.85 **or alternatively $0.15^3 * 0.85^1$**	0.0029 or 0.29%
4 of 4	*Ex: see #1 and see#2 and see #3 and see #4* =0.15 * 0.15 *0.15 * 0.15 =0.15 *0.15*0.15*0.15 **or alternatively $0.15^4 * 0.85^0$**	0.0005or 0.05%

Notice the pattern in the alternative formulas: probability of seeing[# to see] x probability of not seeing[# not to see]. If we let 'p' represent the probability of seeing, this can be written:

$$\textbf{E\#6]} \quad p^k \left(1-p\right)^{n-k}$$

This looks similar to the last part of the BBD formula presented in the introduction. It was partly this similarity which led to combining the beta function with the binomial expansion.

The binomial expansion (multiplying the 'number of ways' with the corresponding probability) is used to create the complete frequency distribution. Let's multiply them together and see if it all works. A correct result will sum to 100% (e.g. summing all the frequency cells should equal 100%):

# Issues	# Ways	Probability (rounded)	Result
0 of 4	1	52.20	52.20
1 of 4	4	9.21	36.85
2 of 4	6	1.63	9.75
3 of 4	4	.29	1.15
4 of 4	1	.05	0.05
TOTAL (based on unrounded probabilities)			100.00

It may have occurred to you that subtracting the 0 cell from 100 gives the proportion of people seeing any issue at least once -- or the reach of the schedule, which is 47.8% rounded. It is the same reach estimate obtained by adding the 1 through 4 frequency cells.

With media formulas from previous exercises, the full specification of the schedule result can be calculated. Recall from the chapter *Basic Marketing and Media Language* that average rating * insertions = Gross Rating Points, so a schedule of 4 issues results in 4 x 15=60 GRPs. GRPs/reach = average frequency, therefore 60/47.8 = 1.3 average frequency. These figures plus the frequency distribution give a pretty complete picture of how this schedule performs.

In summary, we've ended up with a formula that we could use for each frequency cell that looks like this:

$$\textbf{E\#7]} \quad \binom{n}{k} p^k \left(1-p\right)^{n-k} , \text{k=0,1, ... n}$$

Multiple magazines with probability. Basic probability rules can not only be used to estimate reach for multiple issues of a magazine, but can also be used to estimate the combination of schedules in different magazines. Each magazine has a frequency distribution which can be treated as a list of probabilities. Assuming independence again, the estimate of the mix of two publications is calculated by multiplying the probabilities with each other (e.g. 'anding' them). First put one distribution in the rows of a table, and the other in the columns. Then cross-multiply the probabilities and add up the diagonals to get a new frequency distribution— those reading the number of issues in the row *and* those reading the number of issues in the column.

As an example, what would be the result of adding a new magazine, *Us Weekly*, to the four issue schedule of *People*? Assume *Us Weekly* has an average rating of 20.0 percent (or .2). The distribution for the two issue schedule for *Us Weekly* has been calculated the same way as for *People*, and is shown across the top of the table below. The distribution for the 4 issues of *People* is in the rows:

	#		Us Weekly		
			0	1	2
	#	Prob	**0.6400**	**0.3200**	**0.0400**
People	0	**0.5220**	0.3341	0.1670	0.0209
	1	**0.3685**	0.2358	0.1179	0.0147
	2	**0.0975**	0.0624	0.0312	0.0039
	3	**0.0115**	0.0073	0.0037	0.0005
	4	**0.0005**	0.0003	0.0002	0.0000

Each combined cell is calculated by multiplying the row percentage (for *People)* by the column percentage (for *Us Weekly)*. To get the proportion reading 1 *People* AND 1 *Us Weekly*, multiply the probabilities according to the rules: 0.3685 x 0.3200=0.1179 (or about 11.8%). All the other cells are calculated the same way, by multiplying the corresponding row and column percentages. To get the new frequency distribution, 'sum the diagonals' from lower left to upper right (follow the shaded bands), adding all the ways to get a particular frequency level. As an example, there is only one way to not read either publication (33.4%). To have read exactly one of either publication, one could read 1 issue of *People* and none of *Us Weekly* (0.2358) *or* read none of *People* and one of *Us Weekly* (0.1670). These are the only two ways to read exactly one issue in this schedule. As before, sum the probabilities to estimate of the proportion reading only one 0.2358 + 0.1670= 0.4029 or about 40.3%. The full distribution is obtained by adding the other diagonals:

Frequency/ # issues	Proportion
0	0.3341 or 33.4%
1	0.2358 + 0.1670 = 0.4029 or 40.3%
2	0.0624 + 0.1179 + 0.0209 = 0.2012 or 20.1%
3	0.0073 + 0.0312 + 0.0147 = 0.0533 or 5.3%
4	0.0030 + 0.0037+ 0.0039 = 0.0079 or .8%
5	0.0002 +0.0007 = 0.0009 or .1%
6	0.0000 (actually .00002) or .0%

Notice that the 5 and 6 levels are diagonals that aren't labeled in the cross-multiplied table, but are still needed. If the sum of all the cells in the frequency table is 100%, the calculations are correct. Using formulas from previous exercises, the total schedule reach is (100-33.4) = 66.6; GRPs are (4 * 15.0) + (2 * 20) =100 and the average frequency is (100 / 66.6) =1.5.

This process could be extended to three or more publications by putting the result of combining the first two publications as the rows in the cross-multiplication table and putting the distribution of the third publication across the columns and repeating the process.

Adding the Beta Function. So far the discussion has revolved around magazines, but is just as applicable to other media. Average rating works the same whether we're talking about magazines, radio, newspapers, television, etc. Each medium is measured differently, but the 'average rating' concept has a similar meaning for them.

Collecting all the required data and completing all the calculations for mixed media in even a modest media schedule would be a daunting task. A simpler and more generalized way of estimating reach and a frequency distribution is needed—a model. An appropriate model would meet certain criteria, such as:

- Making intuitive sense. A model could be created that *happened* to work, but had no obvious relationship to available data. Such a model would be difficult to explain. Users would always wonder if such a model would continue to work in other situations. And might be impossible to understand and correct strange or improbable results.

- A model should reflect reality as closely as possible. For example, a good model shouldn't be able to produce impossible results, such as a reach greater than 100%, or reach in a medium with no insertions at all.

- A great model would work with a few simple pieces of data that could be easily collected.

We'll soon see that BBD meets these criteria, and that it is a great improvement over simple probability in terms of estimating reach. What we've done so far with probabilities lays the groundwork for the beta binomial function.

Adding the binomial probabilities over all r respondents, gives us an estimated 'average exposure probability' for our media vehicle (that is, the 'average rating'):

$$\text{E\#8]} \quad \binom{n}{k} \sum_{1}^{r} p^k \left(1 - p\right)^{n-k}$$

If we could multiply this by some function 'f', which gave a representation of the average number of ways all the respondents could be exposed, that might get us a reasonable way to estimate an entire schedule. By forcing the total respondents to equal 1 (in other words, each respondent has a 'weight' of 1/r), the result would come out as a decimal fraction, and would always be between 0 and 1. Here's what it would look like:

$$\text{E\#9]} \quad \binom{n}{k} \int_{0}^{1} p^k \left(1 - p\right)^{n-k} f\left(p\right) dp$$

OK, stick with us here. We know it looks a little odd. Since the exposure (reach) estimate needs to be continuous (meaning it can take on any value, not just whole numbers), we switch from summing (Σ) to integration. The $\int$ at the beginning simply means to add up (integrate) the values over all respondents, and the dp at the end means to look at the values in reference to p. Knowing that, the integral 'wrapper' in the rest of the equations can be pretty much ignored; just watch what happens in the middle.

Some really smart marketing mathematicians noticed the similarities between the binomial expansion and the beta function, and thought it might be a good candidate for f(p) which is needed to estimate the 'average number of ways to be exposed to the schedule'. It has all the characteristics we are looking for in a model: it's well-known, well-defined, and well-behaved—it doesn't do 'goofy' things. They thought it might work well—and they were right! We're not going talk about the beta distribution itself much, but here's what it looks like:

$$\text{E\#10] beta distribution} = \frac{p^{a-1}(1-p)^{b-1}}{\beta(a,b)}$$

It's a little confusing, because the beta *distribution* is calculated using the beta *function* in the denominator. They aren't the same. The beta *distribution* is similar in use to the way the 'bell curve' normal distribution is used—the area under the curve is equal to the probability of an event. An important difference between the beta and normal curves is that the normal bell curve shape is defined by a single parameter (the mean), but the beta distribution shape is defined by the two parameters 'a' and 'b,' which allows its shape to vary widely. The β in the denominator stands for 'beta *function*'. The beta *function* in the denominator serves to keep the results on a constant scale.

Putting the beta distribution **E\#10** into the f(p) placeholder in **E\#9,** produces the next equation:

$$\text{E\#11]} \quad \binom{n}{k}\int_0^1 p^k(1-p)^{n-k}\frac{p^{a-1}(1-p)^{b-1}}{\beta(a,b)}dp$$

To simplify, pull the beta *function* denominator out of the integral, and combine like terms:

$$\text{E\#12]} \quad \binom{n}{k}\frac{1}{\beta(a,b)}\int_0^1 p^{k+a-1}(1-p)^{n-k+b-1}dp$$

And there we have it—the beta binomial function that produces the probability of readership, exactly as presented in the heading of the chapter. The term ' $f(k|n,a,b)$ ' in the chapter heading just means 'the reach (exposure) estimate for k given some n, a, and b.' k is the number of spots or insertions or whatever term for exposure units is appropriate for the medium. **E\#12** can be rewritten in a 'user-friendly' form so that the full frequency distribution can easily be calculated:

$$\text{E\#13]} \quad \binom{n}{k}\frac{\beta(a+k,b+n-k)}{\beta(a,b)}$$

This equation will be used in an example, but another form of BBD will make the action of 'a' and 'b' more clear.

Starting again with probability, the average rating can be estimated summing the probabilities over all respondents. Changing from summing to integration for continuous probabilities and setting the total respondents to 1 (again so that each respondent has a weight of 1/r), and using f(p) to estimate the number of ways to be exposed, the result is:

$$\text{E\#14]} \quad \text{Average Rating} = C1 = \int_0^1 pf(p)dp$$

f(p) is a placeholder again for the number of ways into which the beta distribution will be substituted. For convenience later, we're going to call the average rating 'C1', or the cumulative audience for one issue (other terms like 'commercial' or 'insertion' can be used in place of 'issue' where appropriate). Using *or to* estimate the probability of seeing either of the first *two* issues (C2) is kind of messy, as duplication must be removed. Alternatively, it can be calculated using exponents as in **E#6**. This would result in the expression $p^0(1-p)^2$. Since p^0 is always 1, the result becomes $(1-p)^2$ and we could write a new equation similar to **E#14** to estimate the cumulative reach for C2, like this:

$$C2 = \int_0^1 (1-p)^2 f(p)\,dp$$

This idea could extend this to any number of insertions 'n' to calculate the total cumulative reach this way:

$$\textbf{E\#15]}\ Cn = \int_0^1 (1-p)^n f(p)\,dp$$

Now, if we substitute the beta function **E#10** in again for f(p) and simplify, we get this formula for the cumulative reach of n issues:

$$\textbf{E\#16]}\ Cn = 1 - \frac{\beta(a, b+n)}{\beta(a+b)}$$

As with **E#13**, equation **E#16** will be used in an example. First, we'll learn to calculate 'a' and 'b' and what they do. The following equations won't be derived, but all of them are from various forms of equations in this chapter:

$$\textbf{E\#17]}\ \text{sum of a and b } (a+b) = \frac{(C2 - C1)}{C1(1 - C1) - (C2 - C1)}$$

'(a+b)' is first because it is directly calculable from C1 and C2. 'a' is the 'exposure parameter' and you can see it is associated in the exponent with the 'exposed' part (p) of **E#12**. 'b' is the 'non-exposure parameter' associated in the exponent with the 'not exposed' part (1-p) of the same equation. Recall that C1 and C2 are the cumulative proportions exposed to the first (also the average rating) and second issues. These two figures are easily obtained from survey data for individual publications or vehicles. With '(a+b)' in hand, 'a' can be calculated:

$$\textbf{E\#18]}\ \text{exposure parameter 'a'} = (a+b)*C1$$

and 'b' follows:

$$\textbf{E\#19]}\ \text{non-exposure parameter 'b'} = (a+b) - a$$

Taking a moment to reflect here, it should be clear that BBD is the product of the binomial function ('reach' part) and the beta function (the 'how many ways' part). That follows from deriving the BBD formulas by inserting the beta function into the multiplied placeholder f(p), and simplifying the product.

BBD example
Let's work an example using the principles presented so far, and compare the modeled results to actual measurement. Currently no survey company measures the audiences for magazines using physical copies. There are simply too many publications, and physical measurement is very expensive. The major services such as

Chapter 9

Mediamark Research (MRI) and Simmons Market Research Bureau (SMRB) use a technique called 'recent reading' to obtain rating data that is used to model reach. At one time, SMRB did actually measure the audiences of two consecutive issues using physical copies. It would be nice to have a set of physically measured data for half a dozen issues or so to check modeling against.

In the 1950's, *Life* magazine commissioned the Politz company to measure cumulative audiences for 6 consecutive issues of several magazines: *Life, Look, Saturday Evening Post, This Week (a weekly 'Sunday magazine' distributed with newspapers, now defunct), and Ladies Home Journal.* The measured *Post* data from the Politz study can be used to build a BBD model, and then test it to see how well it does. BBD can also be compared to the basic probability methods presented at the beginning of the chapter.

Politz found the following cumulative audiences for *Saturday Evening Post* for persons age 10+ for 6 issues:

# Issues	1	2	3	4	5	6
Cume Reach %	11.8	17.8	21.8	25.0	27.5	29.6

To build a cumulative reach model, estimate the exposure parameters 'a' and 'b' using **E#17, E#18** and **E#19** and the measured values for C1 and C2 *(remember to convert to decimals!):*

$$(a+b) = \frac{(C2-C1)}{C1(1-C1)-(C2-C1)} = \frac{(0.178-0.118)}{0.118(1-0.118)-(0.178-0.118)} = 1.361$$

$$a = (a+b)*C1 = 1.361*0.118 = 0.161$$

$$b = (a+b) - a = 1.361 - 0.161 = 1.200$$

Calculating the beta values. In order to calculate the beta function values we need, use the gammaln() function in *Microsoft Excel. Excel* does have the function betadist() which returns beta density values, but we need a way to calculate the beta *function*, which is a ratio of (yikes!) the gamma function represented by the

symbol 'Γ' $\left(\beta(a,b) = \frac{\Gamma(a)\Gamma(b)}{\Gamma(a+b)} \right)$.

A formula for the beta function that can be used in Excel is:

E#20] β(a,b)=exp(gammaln(a)+gammaln(b)-gammaln(a + b))

Gammaln() takes the natural log of the gamma function and allows the use of addition and subtraction operators instead of division and multiplication. It also turns out that the gamma function for integers is factorial (for integers, $\Gamma(n) = (n-1)!, n > 0$).

Logarithms help avoid potential problems like overflowing the processor (175! is too large for many computers to compute, but 175 would be a relatively small number of insertions in a media schedule). *Exp()* (exponentiation) is used to convert the logarithm answer back to the desired result.

With a way to calculate the beta function, **E#16** can be used to model the cumulative reach for 6 issues of the *Saturday Evening Post.* Since the estimates for 'a' and 'b' came directly from the measurement data for C1 and C2, the reach estimate for the first two issues will match exactly. Here's the math worked out for the first issue:

Numerator :

$\beta(a, \mathbf{b+n})$ *from Excel* = exp(gammaln(a)+gammaln(**b+n**)-gammaln(a+**b+n**))
=exp(gammaln(0.161)+gammaln(**1.200+1**)-gammln(0.161+**1.200+1**)) = 5.264

Important! *Notice that in the numerator, 'b+n' is used for 'b' every time! If you do not make this substitution where required in the beta function you will get an incorrect result.*

Denominator:

$\beta(a,b)$ *from Excel* = exp(gammaln(a)+gammaln(b)-gammaln(a+b))
= exp(gammaln(0.161)+ gammaln(1.200)-gammaln(0.161+1.200)) = 5.969

$$C1 = 1 - \frac{\beta(a,b+1)}{\beta(a+b)} = 1 - \frac{5.264}{5.969} = 1 - 0.882 = 0.118 \, or \, 11.8\%$$

The cumulative reach for each of the remaining successive issues is calculated the same way, substituting the correct number of issues for 'n' each time. Here are all 6 issue results compared to the measured values:

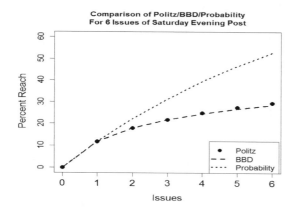

Comparison of Politz/BBD/Probability
For 6 Issues of Saturday Evening Post

	Cume Reach		
Issues	**Politz Study**	**BBD Model**	**Probability**
1	11.8	11.8	11.8
2	17.8	17.8	22.2
3	21.8	21.7	31.4
4	25.0	24.6	39.5
5	27.5	26.9	46.6
6	29.6	28.7	52.9

Notice the BBD model reach estimates are quite close to the tabulated values. Commercial programs used in agencies make minor tweaks to further improve the fit. The basic probability estimates are also shown in the table and graph—and rapidly stray from the measured estimates. BBD does much better because it uses more information, and does not assume independence (e.g. BBD can accommodate duplication that is not random, whereas the assumption of random duplication is explicit in basic probability—when removing the duplication back in **E#3**, the $(p_1 * p_2)$ estimate of duplication assumes randomness because the two events are assumed independent).

Let's try calculating the frequency distribution for six issues. The sum of the exposure cells 1 through 6 must total the 28.7% (cumulative reach) estimated for the six issues, so that figure can be used to verify the results.

E#13 can be used to calculate the entire frequency distribution:

$$\text{Read k of n issues} = \binom{n}{k} \frac{\beta(a+k, b+n-k)}{\beta(a,b)}$$

'a' and 'b' are already calculated, so the rest of the equation can be worked easily. *n* and *k* are the total number of issues and frequency level respectively. Here's how to calculate 'read 1 of 6 issues:'

First, figure out the combination part, $\binom{n}{k}$:

$$\binom{n}{k} = \frac{n!}{k!(n-r)!} = \frac{6!}{1!(6-1)!} = 6$$

Note that *Microsoft Excel* can calculate the combinations for you. The *Excel* function to use is *combin(n,k)*. For 1 of 6 issues, use '=combin(6,1)' that is, 'six issues taken one at a time.'

Calculate the numerator β(a+k, b+n-k). ***Important:*** *substitute 'a+k' for 'a' and 'b+n-k' for 'b' in the numerator:*

β***(a+k, b+n-r)*** *from Excel* = exp(gammaln(***a+k***)+gammaln(***b+n-r***)-gammaln(***a+k+b+n-r***))
=exp(gammaln(***0.161+ 1***)+gammaln(***1.200+6-1***)-gammln(***0.161+ 1+1.200+6-1***)) = .110

And of course, β*(a,b)* = 5.969 is already calculated.

So those reading exactly 1 of 6 issues is:

$$6 * \frac{0.110}{5.969} = 0.111 \, or \, 11.1\%$$

Here is the full distribution worked out using **E#13**:

k	n!/k!(nk)!	β(a+k,b+n-k)	β(a,b)	Proportion Reading k of n
0	1	4.255		0.713
1	6	0.110		0.111
2	15	0.025		0.062
3	20	0.013	5.969	0.042
4	15	0.012		0.031
5	6	0.024		0.024
6	1	0.102		0.016
			Total	1.000

The sum of all the frequency cells ads to 1.0 (100%) as it should, and the total exposed (sum of cells 1 through 6) is 0.287 (28.7%) which is also correct.

Conclusion

Hopefully by now you have a general idea of how BBD was developed from basic probability. While it's possible to estimate reach and frequency with probability for an entire schedule, we've seen that simple probability quickly deviates from measured data. It is also becomes unwieldy for even a modest schedule. Imagine trying to estimate reach for a schedule that had even just 5 magazines with 3 insertions apiece, 10 television programs with 5 insertions and 4 radio networks with 10 insertions each. This is a trivial schedule, but the number of calculations required to define the results is enormous and burdensome.

BBD allows us to 'short circuit' this process. We've used it to understand how to estimate reach and a frequency distribution for a single vehicle, but the application to a schedule of multiple media is somewhat instinctive. If we could work out a kind of 'average rating' for the schedule, and then estimate the exposure parameters 'a' and 'b', then BBD could be used to estimate reach and frequency estimates at any weight level we might choose, using the relatively simple equations in this chapter.

Estimating the average C1 and C2 values for a large data set so 'a' and 'b' can be calculated for BBD applications can be quite complicated. However, it is possible to estimate 'a' and 'b' without a C2 if reach is known for a second higher weight level. This is done is using a computer to 'guess and refine'. Initial values for 'a' and 'b' are estimated using the average rating, then an estimate for reach at the second point (often obtained from test schedule tabulations) is calculated. Comparing the calculated result to the actual second point indicates how to modify 'a' and 'b' so that the estimates approach the known second point. Eventually the estimate matches the second point or is close enough to stop.

Though this description is fairly straightforward, it is computationally complicated and is facilitated by programming, so we won't be doing a computational example. However, this is the method used internally by MFP (and commercial programs) to build reach curves. Estimates for the exposure parameters have been calculated in MFP for all the demographic cells. Each time a GRP weight level is entered for a medium, reach is estimated for each selected cell in the target demographic and then the results from all the cells are combined to get the reach estimate for the specific target.

Combining the frequency distributions using BBD is more complicated than the process of combining magazines with probability, but the idea is very similar, and we won't go through it here.

Finally, BBD can be expressed in several forms, each of which leads to different methods of calculating 'a' and 'b', but the results are always the same. We've chosen methods that maintain consistency with the form of BBD presented at the beginning of the chapter.

Acknowlegements: This is a complicated subject. We'd like to acknowledge a readable but quite thorough layman's discussion of this topic, *Readership Research and Computers* © 1985 by Paul Sumner, published by Newsweek International. This chapter follows the general approach taken there, but is simplified greatly and skips many details. The data used in the BBD example in this chapter and the exercise that follows come from *A Study of Four Media*, conducted for *Life* magazine in 1952/53 by Alfred Politz Research.

UNIVERSITY MEDIA PLAN: SYRACUSE UNIVERSITY

Each new edition of Media Flight Plan highlights a student-created media plan judged by the authors as an excellent excellent example of university-level scholarship.

It is usefull to have a model of excellence to follow when attempting a new project or assignment. Included here are two summary pages of the Tim Tam case written by students at Syracuse University.

Thanks to students Mike Friedman and Jin Maekawa and their advisor Amy Faulkner for permission to include their case as an excellent example of critical thinking and strategic media planning.

In addition to excellent writing and analysis, these students took the time to export their flowchart and other data from MFP and formatted it to integrate well into their writeup.

You can find the full case on the MFP website:

1. Log on to mediaflightplan.com
2. Click [Ground School]
3. Scroll down and click on [Syracuse Tim Tam Case]

Situational Analysis:

Product

Pepperidge Farm is introducing a new product line of indulgent chocolate biscuits into the US market. Two layers of chocolate malted biscuit, a light chocolate crème filling and an outer coat of chocolate make up a TimTam, a ready-to-eat cookie that carries cult-like status in Australia and New Zealand (Newell, 2013). TimTam will be added to a strong line of Pepperidge Farm cookies to boost performance in the Baking and Snacking Division of Campbell's International, the parent company.

Place

The TimTam brand was made available at Target stores in a limited number of major metro markets, but Pepperidge Farm aims to roll the cookies out on a national scale. Pepperidge Farm distributes its products in all major national and regional grocery stores, including cookies ranging from Milano to Chessmen, and soon, TimTam.

Price

During the limited Target store release in 2009-2010, one 7oz. package of TimTam cost $3.39, aligned with average cookie package costs like OREO ($2.99-$3.99). Target frequently sold TimTam for the price of $2.50 on sale or offered other price promotions. However, standard cookies like OREO come with 30 cookies (439g) and TimTam only come with 11 biscuits (200g). Because of this price-quantity relationship, the brand's foreign reputation, and the Pepperidge Farm labeling, TimTam will be perceived as a more premium snack cookie.

Promotion

The most recent promotional effort from Pepperidge Farm regarding TimTam was via Facebook in the winter of 2012. The TimTam Cookies page (US) has 21,630 likes and has outdated contest and coupon promotions from the limited release in Target stores. One effort included a printable $1-off coupon in December of 2010 as a holiday push (Livesey, 2010). Pepperidge Farm also collaborated with Gail Simmons, a judge on Bravo's show Top Chef, when TimTam first launched in 2009. During the introductory launch, consumers and TimTam fanatics were encouraged to share their thoughts via photos and videos on www.ILoveTimTamCookies.com. One lucky winner was selected each month and received a TimTam-themed party pack from Pepperidge Farm. Social media buzz was a centerpiece to the campaign during NYC sampling events and Australian-themed restaurants and bars leading into the holiday season.

TimTam Positioning:

Brand Perceptual Map: Price vs. Sophistication

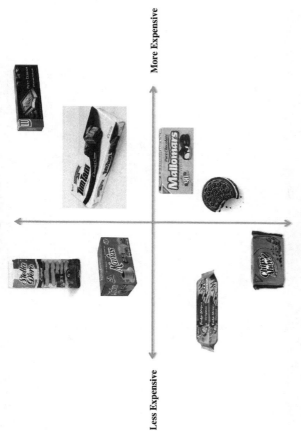

Considering the factors of price and sophistication, there is room in the market for TimTam to gain unique positioning. While in terms of value per pack, TimTam would be considered on the more expensive side (see Price on pg. 1), it garners a more sophisticated perception. Because of the brands imported connotations, along with the practice of consuming TimTam with coffee or hot drinks, pushed the biscuit towards an older crowd. Unlike Keebler and Chips Ahoy!, TimTam is less appropriate for kids and has an implied level of indulgence only an adult could recognize. Brands like LU Petit Écolier, while highly sophisticated, can cost upwards of $4.50 per pack with a smaller sized biscuit than TimTam. Cookies marketed with as an affordable indulgence can help consumers achieve a slice of luxury while remaining within their budgets (Frank, 2013).

Target Audience:

Meet Cassandra:

Cassandra Johnson is a 29-year-old single woman living in New York City with her roommate Lauren. She is employed at a Public Relations firm in Manhattan representing artists and musicians making $68,000 a year and is striving for a promotion that will earn her a decent raise. In between traveling with her clients and working in the office, she often finds herself spending her free time hanging out with her friends and exploring new parts of the city. Cassandra is a fairly health conscious person, goes to the gym regularly and eats well. However, she does believe in treating herself with something indulgent every now and then. She doesn't like eating mass quantities of snacks, because she would much rather have a couple pieces of something sweet and really enjoying the treat rather than eating tons of junk. In the future, Cassandra sees herself settling down but is still driven to move forward in her career.

Demographics	Primary Target	Secondary Target
Gender	Female	
Age	25-49	25-34
County Size	County Size A	
Education	High School Graduate	College Graduate
Income	>$30,000	>$50,000
Marital Status	Any	Single
Employment	Mostly Professional/Technical, Office and Administrative	
Lifestyle	Generally busy, on-the-go media consumer, lives near a metropolitan area, independent, socially active, regular user of public transportation	

Media Mix Strategy:

National Media	Raise general awareness of brand launch with targeted reach
	The target audience is constantly on the go, and therefore TimTam advertising requires a media plan that will allow them to be reached accordingly. Many media selections are focused on the modern commuter, and all selections are portable media, a decision made clear by the absence of television (almost) completely. Additional spot budget in 7 markets aims to boost winter sales of Pepperidge Farm with holiday themed campaigns (and sales promotions), with R/F levels as high as 90/5.0 among women 25-49. Because the TimTam launch will introduce the brand to Americans who have never tasted the cookie, spurring trial is an extra consideration threaded throughout the media mix objectives.
Network Radio: Drive Time	While women 25-34 are more likely to live in a city, the older half of the target is likely commuting into work from the suburbs or the town over. Morning and evening radio will aim to raise general awareness of the TimTam release and influence top-of-mind purchase during the weekly evening trip to the grocery store.
Print: Women's Magazines	Not only is the target very receptive to magazine advertising, but print ads with wisely-written copy can speak to the emotional appeal of indulging in a TimTam at the end of a long day. Sexy, high quality, color ads will describe the decadence and luxury that the target feels she deserves.
Internet: Paid Social Media	Pepperidge Farm is well behind its competitors in terms of internet presence and social media share-of-voice. Paid social media promotions will not only raise awareness of the brand in the US, but allow a community of TimTam fanatics to start an organic conversation about the brand launch.
Internet: Targeted Sites	Well-placed internet advertising will allow target consumers to actively discover the TimTam brand for themselves. By running copy in digital format, banner ads will also coincide with ongoing social media efforts and contribute to word of mouth sharing.

Spot Media	Build on national plan with increased frequency and sales promotions
Spot TV: Cable	30-second television commercials in 7 spot markets will cross-promote the "TimTam Home for the Holidays," a fan contest with a chance to win an all-expense paid trip to Australia, the homeland of the beloved biscuit treat. Along with spot radio, targeted cable commercials will aim to connect TimTam with a cultured, sophisticated target psychographic on appropriate cable programming.
Spot Radio: Drive Time	Similar to the national radio strategy, spot commercials during drive time will aim to add frequency by reaching daily commuters. Entertaining and Australian-inspired radio spots will aim to give a fading Pepperidge Farm brand a spark in spot markets with comparatively low BDIs.
Outdoor: Transit / Urban	Transit advertisements on buses, taxis and out-of-home fixtures will aim to reach the target on the go. Starting in September and throughout the winter, outdoor ads will remind the target that indulgence in just a 20-minute subway ride away.

Year At A Glance:

	Reach		Average Frequency		GRPs			$(000)		
	Goal	Est	Goal	Est	Goal	Est	Balance	Goal	Est	Balance
August	65	68.7	2.5	2.4	163	162	0	1048.6	879.0	169.5
September	75	80.0	3.5	3.0	263	237	25	1693.8	1727.7	-33.9
October	80	83.5	4.0	3.5	320	295	25	2064.8	2032.8	32.1
November	85	84.6	4.0	3.7	340	315	25	2193.9	2196.0	-2.1
December	90	89.7	5.0	4.7	450	425	25	2903.7	2716.8	186.8
January	90	89.7	5.0	4.7	450	425	25	2903.7	2716.8	186.8
February	85	84.5	4.0	3.7	340	315	25	2193.9	2130.7	63.2
March	75	75.5	3.0	2.7	225	200	25	1451.8	1772.8	-321.0
April	65	69.3	2.5	2.3	163	162	0	1048.6	1314.0	-265.5
May	0	0.0	0.0	0.0	0	0	0	0.0	0.0	0.0
June	0	0.0	0.0	0.0	0	0	0	0.0	0.0	0.0
July	0	0.0	0.0	0.0	0	0	0	0.0	0.0	0.0
Total					2712.5	2536	0	17502.8	17468.7	16.1
National Contingency $(000)										250.0
Spot Contingency $(000)										107.0

Section II

Media Flight Plan
Exercises

IMPRESSIONS AND RATINGS

Learning Objective:

Impressions and ratings are the most basic measurement tools in media planning, and although both tell us the same thing, each provides a unique way of expressing audience size. Think of ratings and impressions as universal media planning tools that play vital roles in measuring most all media.

We Don't Measure Ad audiences

We don't measure ad audiences– we measure audiences for media vehicles that carry ads. Impressions are commonly thought of as counting "eyeballs on the medium." (e.g., counting the number of people who tune in to *60 Minutes* or buy *People* magazine). It's important to clarify that we are not talking about "eyeballs on advertisements" in *People* or on *60 Minutes*. That's because we don't currently measure ad audience. Instead, we measure the audience for the media vehicles that carry the ads. For example, assume we run an ad for Mercedes Benz C-Class Coupe on Sixty Minutes, and 1.8 million persons tune in to *60 Minutes*. We cannot claim 1.8 million persons saw our ad. In truth, 1.8 million people only had an opportunity to see the ad (were "exposed" as in exposed to a virus – they may or may not "catch" it), because rarely does anyone "catch" all sixty minutes of *60 Minutes*. Keep in mind that "exposure" and "impression" are often used interchangeably. Technically they aren't the same, but in every-day advertising talk, both are used to indicate opportunity to see. We note that many agencies now use "commercial minute ratings" which are an improvement over program ratings, but are still not true exposure. Rather, they are the average of minutes with commercial content, weighted by the number of commercial seconds (e.g. a minute with 3 seconds of commercial content has a weight of 3, while a minute with 56 seconds has a weight of 56).

Table I shows the audiences (in impressions) for several TV programs:

Table I (Universe for Adults 18-49 = 122.9 million)		
Program	**Network**	**Adult 18-49 Imp (000)**
Castle	ABC	14140
CBS Evening News	CBS	13650
Monday Night Football	ESPN	7750
Tonight Show	NBC	5900
30 Minute Meals	FOOD	490
White Collar	USA	1360

Note how impressions are shown in thousands (000), the most common way impressions are reported. There are a couple of reasons for this. One is that the precision of measurement for most media requires rounding at this level. Another is that even for programs with small audiences, it's still a big number, and it's unwieldy. When calculating with impressions, be sure all the numbers you work with are expressed on the same scale, i.e., – in the same numeric format. Often it will be necessary to **add the zeros** (i.e. multiply by 1000 if shown in "000") to make sure all numbers are expressed in the same way.

Example problem: Impressions can be added together to indicate the total "weight" of an advertising schedule. Your client, *Orbit* chewing gum, has agreed to run a schedule consisting of 3 spots on *Castle*, and 12 spots on *Rachael Ray's 30 Minute Meals*. How many impressions – reporting the complete number in thousands – will this schedule generate? Remember: **Complete number = numbers reported with all digits showing, including all zeros**.

Solving for Impressions: Each spot generates the impressions reported for that program. The first step is to figure the **total impressions for each program**. Next, sum the impressions for all programs in the schedule to get the **total impressions for the schedule**. See example in Table II:

Table II
3 spots on *Castle* x 14,140 = 42,420 (000) impressions + 12 spots on *30 Minute Meals* x 490 = 5,880 (000) impressions Total for schedule: 48,300 (000) impressions Don't forget to multiply by 1000 to get the **complete number**: 48,300 x 1000 = **48,300,000** or 48.3 million impressions

GROSS = Duplication or Multiple Opportunities to See
The total for the ad schedule in Table II would be expressed as 48.3 million *gross* impressions. The term *gross* is applied to situations where there is a chance that a person will have *more than one opportunity to see* an ad. And, since most target audiences get multiple exposures, we call this *duplication*. In our example there was a total of 15 spots – opportunities – for an individual to see an ad running in two TV programs, *Castle* and *30 Minute Meals*. Because a person could see more than one spot in either of these two programs, or could see a spot in both, we must assume duplication and the result is gross impressions. Rule of thumb: The term *gross* infers *duplication*, and duplication infers *multiple exposures*.

Ratings: Easier to Grasp than Impressions
Some media professionals call impressions "boxcar numbers" since they are so unwieldy. Impressions alone don't communicate much information, and using huge numbers verbally or in writing gets awkward. For example, knowing a spot on *Tonight Show* produces 5,900,000 impressions among adults 18-49 doesn't give us a sense of proportion. Knowing what **part or percentage** of the target audience was exposed is much easier to grasp than 5,900,000 impressions. If we factor in the universe of Adults 18-49, then we'll know what **percentage** of the target was exposed (had the "opportunity to see"). Here's the formula for calculating a rating:

$$\text{Rating} = \frac{\text{Impressions (000)}}{\text{Universe (000)}} \times 100$$

Note that both universe and impressions must be expressed in the same numeric format; **often they are NOT** and you must change one or both numbers to get the right answer. This formula will also work if impressions and the universe are in complete numbers. Once again: **Complete number = numbers reported with all digits showing, including all zeros**. For example, in Table III, the **complete number** expression for **Universe Adults 18-49 is 122,900,000**.

Example problem: The *universe* is often reported in *millions*. In the subheading below Table III, note how **Universe for Adults 18-49** is reported as **122.9 million**, but here you also encounter **122,900** when reported in numeric units of thousands (both are common). For example, look carefully at *Castle*. Note how the rating is calculated using Adult 18-49 Imp 000 (**14140**) and universe (**122900**) reported in thousands despite the **122.9** million reported in the heading. This table works because in the math section, *both impressions and universe are expressed in the same numeric units* (in this case NOT adding zeros) when calculated. Pay close attention here – depending on how the data is reported, you may need to add zeros or not add zeros to keep numeric units the same.

Table III (Universe for Adults 18-49 = 122.9 million)							
Program	**Network**	**Adult 18-49 Imp (000)**					**Rating**
Castle	ABC	14140	/	122900	x 100	=	11.5
CBS Evening News	CBS	13650	/	122900	x 100	=	11.1
Monday Night Football	ESPN	7750	/	122900	x 100	=	6.3
Tonight Show	NBC	5900	/	122900	x 100	=	4.8
30 Minute Meals	FOOD	490	/	122900	x 100	=	0.4
White Collar	USA	1360	/	122900	x 100	=	1.1

Gross Impressions vs. Gross Rating

The term *gross impression* indicates the possibility of multiple impressions (duplication) per target member, i.e., - being exposed to an ad more than once in different vehicles, or more than once in the same vehicle. The concept of gross rating is much the same as gross impressions; if duplication is possible, we get *gross ratings*, but as always with ratings, the number is converted to a percentage. If only one opportunity to see is possible, they are just ratings or *net* ratings. Like impressions, **ratings can be added together as long as they are for the same target audience.** When this is done, ratings also become "gross" and are typically called *Gross Rating Points*, or *GRPs* for short. The acronym is pronounced in different ways, "G-R-P's" and "Gurps" are perhaps the most frequent; you'll also hear "Grips." Some ad agencies make a further distinction by reserving the term Gross Rating Points to be used only when measuring households. Moreover, particular targets or demographics are distinguished as "Target Rating Points" or TRPs. This is simply a convention; there is no difference in definition between the two other than one is used for households and other for a specific target audience. You'll see both used interchangeably.

Problems

Table IV provides data for most of the problems in this exercise:

Table IV Women 25-54 Universe: 116.82 MM [116,820 (000)]		
Program	**Network**	**Women 25-54 Imp (000)**
Good Morning America	ABC	1520
Regis & Kelly	Syndication	4090
60 Minutes	CBS	12618
The Mentalist	CBS	11683
HBO Movie	HBO	351

1) Report the impressions for *Good Morning America*, *Regis & Kelly*, and *HBO Movie* as **complete numbers**. What simple math step is necessary to make the conversion?

2) Your client, *Emeril's Original Essence* and a dozen other labels, (brand licensed by Emeril's Food of Love Productions) has decided to use your recommended TV schedule for the winter season:

Good Morning America	**4 spots**
The Mentalist	**3 spots**
HBO Movie	**12 spots**

Emeril's has decided to report the **total impressions** number – based on the TV schedule in Table IV – as part of a promotional brochure targeted at their sales reps and wholesalers so they know how well Emeril's spices, sauces and marinades will be supported. What number will you give them to place in their brochure? Tip: Create a table above – first calculate impressions for *each* program, and then sum the *total impressions* for the complete TV schedule. Show your math.

3) In preparing your recommendation, you'll need to calculate the rating for each of the programs you considered in Table IV. Calculate the rating for each program and show your math.

Good Morning America

Regis & Kelly

60 Minutes

The Mentalist

HBO Movie

4) How many total Gross Rating Points (GRPs) will be generated by the advertising schedule in problem 2? Tip: You just finished calculating the ratings for these programs, so most of the work is done.

5) You've been working with a new media person who works in the client's corporate headquarters. She recently graduated with from an ivy-league MBA school, but was never exposed to media planning.

A. She noticed that you use the terms "gross rating" and "gross impression," and wants to know the definition for each. Explain each in your own words (Tip: you can refer to the text part of this exercise.)

B. She is also confused on another issue. She thinks *impressions* for an ad in a TV program indicate how many people will actually see the ad. Explain this in your own words.

6) Which will add more gross rating points (GRPs) to a schedule: 6 spots in *Regis & Kelly* or 2 spots in *60 Minutes*? Show math to support your decision.

7. The *Castle* TV program rating for Women 25-54 last month was 12.8. Calculate the impressions for *Castle* and show your math. Tip: impressions(000) = rating(000)/100 * universe(000)

GROSS RATING POINTS, REACH AND FREQUENCY

Learning Objective

It's important to understand the direct mathematical relationship between reach, frequency and gross rating points. This relationship allows marketers to determine what proportion of their target audience is being reached and how often the average audience member has an "opportunity to see." Understanding this relationship forms the foundation for media schedule analysis and comparison.

Impressions and Rating Points

Recall that a rating is the number of impressions generated – divided by the universe – and finally multiplied by 100. For example, if you could buy one commercial on a special show that reached each target audience member exactly once, then the rating for that show would be a perfect 100, and the impressions generated would be exactly the same as the universe. In real media life, we have to buy many spots, and reach some target members more than once, and others not at all. So 100 rating points is the same number of impressions as the population, but is not the same as reaching 100 percent of the population. One rating point is equivalent to the number of impressions in one percent of the population (universe):

$$\text{one rating point} = \frac{\text{universe}}{100} = \text{\# impressions equal to one percent of the universe}$$

A gross rating point for **different targets** will equal a different number of impressions, because each target has a different universe or base. Like fractions with different denominators that can't be added, **GRPs for different targets cannot be added either**.

Gross rating points can be converted to impressions and back again with the following formulas:

$$\frac{\text{GRPs}}{100} \times \text{universe} = \text{impressions}$$

$$\frac{\text{impressions}}{\text{universe}} \times 100 = \text{GRPs}$$

Solving for impressions

Example Problem: Your latest media planning masterpiece – a magazine schedule – generates 143 GRPs against a target of 11.9 million adults who regularly play board games. How many impressions does this plan generate?

From the discussion above, you know that 100 rating points is the number of impressions equal to the universe. You can use the formula provided above to calculate the number of impressions. Many people find it easier to convert universe figures provided in millions (MM or '0,000) or thousands ('000) to whole numbers before solving the problem. This is done by multiplying the universe by 1,000,000 or 1,000 respectively:

$$11.9 \times 1,000,000 = 11,900,000 \text{ impressions}$$

$$\frac{143}{100} \times 11,900,000 = 17,017,000 \text{ impressions, or 17.0 MM}$$

We round numbers for convenience—the answer would likely be reported as "about 17 million impressions."

Exercise 2

You can calculate how many gross rating points result from a schedule by adding the ratings for each ad. That total can be converted to gross impressions to demonstrate how many total *opportunities to see* occurred. Both of these give us some idea of total weight, but neither tells us how many people were potentially exposed—that is, how many people had *at least one* opportunity to see, regardless of how many opportunities or impressions they received. *The net number of target persons "exposed" at least once is called REACH.* The TV schedule below illustrates the *vital relationship between gross rating points and reach.*

Cable TV reruns of *Monk* provide 4 impressions to B, D, F, and H. The rating for *Monk* is 40 (4 persons with an opportunity to see out of 10 persons in the universe times 100). *Evening News* "exposes" A, B, and C, and has a rating of 30 (3 persons divided by 10 persons in the universe times 100), and by the same process, *Survivor* has a rating of 50.

	A	B	C	D	E	F	G	H	I	J
Monk		■		■		■		■		
Evening News	■	■	■							
Survivor		■			■	■		■		■

Remember: Gross Means Duplication or Multiple Opportunities to See

If the ratings are added together, the schedule produces 120 gross rating points, or 12 gross impressions. Once totaled, the schedule turns gross delivering *gross impressions* and *gross rating points*. For example, persons B, F and H had multiple opportunities to see multiple programs. But if each program is considered alone, ratings and impressions are not gross because each person has only one opportunity to see that program. Example: Survivor gets 50% rating – *and no duplication* – because persons B, E, F, H, and J had *only one opportunity to see* Survivor.

"Impressions" is commonly used as an abbreviation for "Gross Impressions."

As discussed earlier, in theory it is possible for impressions to be UNduplicated. However, in practice impressions are almost always gross (duplicated) when applied to a real world media plan. That's why it is common to see the term "impressions" used without "gross" preceding it.

Reach Formula

Reach = Net number of target persons "exposed" at least once

Notwithstanding all of the media weight in this schedule, we were not able to *reach* (provide an opportunity to see) every person in the target. Count them – only 8 of the 10 received at least one impression. Our schedule, therefore, has a reach of 80. The formula for reach is:

$$\text{reach} = \frac{\text{target audience with opportunities to see ("exposed")}}{\text{target audience}} \times 100$$

Solving for Reach & GRPs

Example Problem: Suppose the client can only afford *Monk* and *Evening News*. What's the reach for this shortened schedule, and how many GRPs are generated? First, note that six persons (A, B, C, D, F, and H) are exposed by *Monk, Evening News* or both.

6 Persons Exposed ÷ Universe of 10 Persons = .06 X 100 = 60 Reach

Rating for Monk = 40 (4 out of 10 exposed); Rating for Evening News = 30

40 + 30 = 70 Gross Rating Points

Calculating both Reach & Frequency (See Pictograph)

While eight of the target population had at least one opportunity for exposure, some had more. B is a heavy viewer—and was exposed to each program. Others, like F and H were exposed twice, and some, like A, only once. We can calculate the average number of times each target member had an opportunity to see by dividing the total number of impressions by the number reached. The result is called "average frequency." In this example:

12 impressions* (total persons exposed) ÷ 8 Persons Reached = 1.5 Average Frequency

Here's an example where the term "impressions" may be used in practice, but it actually means "gross impressions." Why are the 12 impressions in this equation actually gross?

This same calculation works with gross rating points and reach, which are impressions expressed as percentages: 120/80=1.5 (recall, from the formula in exercise 1: 12 impressions/10 universe x 100 = 120 gross rating points; and 8 exposed/10 universe x 100 = 80 reach).

Reach, average frequency (often shortened to just 'frequency') and gross rating points are all related this way:

Memorize this formula: Reach x Average Frequency = Gross Rating Points

If you know either of the two values, you can calculate the third. To calculate reach or frequency, you can use these algebraic equivalents:

$$\text{Avg Freq} = \frac{\text{GRPs}}{\text{Reach}} \quad \text{and} \quad \text{Reach} = \frac{\text{GRPs}}{\text{Avg Freq}}$$

This is one of the most important mathematical relationships in media. With it you can estimate the weight needed to achieve goals, and understand the exposure pattern of the average person in the target audiences.

Problems

1. How many impressions are in one gross rating point for each target? First, convert target data to complete numbers, and then divide by 100.

Target	Universe (MM)	X	÷	= Impressions
Adults 25-54	116.82	_____	_____	_____
Women 18-49	62.66	_____	_____	_____
Men 65+	13.88	_____	_____	_____

2. Your campaign for Kellogg's Frosted Mini-Wheats, positioned as a "lightly sweetened whole grain wheat alternative" for kids, is primarily targeted to children 6-14. It is hoped kids will request the breakfast "bite size confection" from their parents. The secondary target is mothers of young children. The campaign has elements of fun to attract young children, but health overtones directed at mothers. Your campaign results in 300 GRPs for children 6-14, and 240 GRPs for the secondary target, mothers. The reach for the two targets is 85 and 78 respectively. What is the average frequency for each target?

3) Your target audience is children age 6-14. Communication objectives for the next media flight call for these minimums:

 • Reach: 80%
 • Average frequency: 6

 Calculate the minimum gross rating points required for this set of objectives.

4. In Question 3, will all children reached (age 6-14) get 6 impressions? You need more than a yes/no answer. Explain the "why" behind your answer.

ALL REMAINING QUESTIONS RELATE TO THE PICTOGRAPH BELOW
Assume your media plan includes magazine schedule targeted to men age 18-34.

	A	B	C	D	E	F	G	H
	😊	😊	😊	😊	😊	😊	😊	😊
Car & Driver		■		■	■	■		
GQ		■	■		■			
Bicycling					■	■		■

5. What is the universe for men 18-34 in this magazine schedule? (Tip: Count the smiley faces)

6. Calculate the rating for *each* publication. (Rating = Target Exposed ÷ Universe X 100)
Remember, ratings are expressed as percents.

      Car & Driver   _____

      GQ   _____

      Bicycling   _____

7. How many total gross rating points (GRPs) are generated by the whole magazine schedule?

      Car & Driver   _____

      GQ   _____

      Bicycling   _____

      Total GRPs: _____

8. How many gross impressions does each magazine generate? Total gross impressions?

      Car & Driver   _____

      GQ   _____

      Bicycling   _____

      Total Gross Impressions: _____

9. Calculate the reach for this magazine schedule, and show your math.

10. Calculate average frequency for this magazine schedule, and show your math.

ONLINE EXPERIMENT: GRPs, REACH AND FREQUENCY

Registration and Logging In . . .Do this before starting Exercise on next page

1. Get your *MFP* Access Code – it's located on the inside front cover of this book. Carefully scratch off the silver coating with the edge of a coin.
2. Open your internet browser.
3. Go to: **www.mediaflightplan.com**
4. Click **[New User Registration]** just under **Login** top of screen.
5. Follow registration instructions. You'll need your access code to log in the first time.
6. Once finished with registration, log in.
7. Begin the experiments below.

Objective: At this point you should be familiar with the theoretical and mathematical underpinnings of reach, frequency and GRPs. Now it's time to apply your theoretical knowledge with a hands-on experiment. All three experiments use the *Media Flight Plan* program.

Syndicated media measurement services typically measure exposure to specific vehicles—programs for television, average issue audience for magazines, average quarter hour audience for radio, gross impressions for internet, etc. Planners usually don't know which programs or websites they will be using during the planning stages of a campaign, so models must be employed to estimate parameters like reach, GRPs and average frequency. Hopefully, while working through exercises 1 and 2, you discovered that duplication is a major issue in estimating reach. We cannot estimate reach without knowing how much duplication is generated in each media buy. Many millions are spent in measuring media, but measuring the myriad ways duplication happens in every conceivable media schedule is virtually impossible. Reach is usually modeled from GRPs in commercial media programs, and the basic formula (GRPs = Reach x Frequency . . . using the algebraic relationship between these three media pillars) is used to derive the average frequency. Sophisticated models allow media planners to estimate the *frequency distribution* which shows how many persons are exposed at each possible frequency level in a schedule.

Fortunately, you don't have to be a statistics genius to be a planning genius—computer programs are much faster at doing such calculations than humans, and good planners can learn how to interpret the results even if they are not the world's greatest mathematicians. A good analogy is the way we use cars. Most of us could not build an engine, let alone explain the internal workings. But we have learned that with the proper input – gasoline and a key – and how to manipulate the input – accelerator, steering wheel, etc., we can transport ourselves from point A to point B. In our journeys, we learn that there is a relationship between speed, time and distance. The same kind of relationship exists with reach, frequency, and gross rating points: If one of the variables is held constant say distance (or GRPs) then as speed (or reach) increases or decreases, time (or frequency) must do the exact opposite to balance the relationship.

To continue this exercise, go to www.mediaflightplan.com, log in, and follow the instructions below.

Start the MFP Program by clicking **[Launch MFP]** on the screen.

Note that your screen might look a bit different depending on your computer or browser, but the information displayed should be the same.

On the right side of the screen, you'll see a a row of buttons, starting with one labeled **Target Audience**. Click it, and in the dialog box that appears, click **[Adults]**, then the age groups **25-34**, **35-49**, and **50-54** as shown in the figure below. The "Current Demo" box should be green and read "Adults ages 25-54". Click **[OK]**.

In the **Target Demographic Updated** dialog box that follows, leave the default option selected and click **[OK]**. You should now be back at the main screen.

Now focus on the main screen. Observe the headings—from left to right, Medium, Ad Type, Unit Cost, Units, and Ext Cost. In this exercise, you will be typing only in the Units column. It's circled in the graphic below. (Caution: If your cursor wanders into the Unit Cost column, you'll get wrong answers). The Ad Type column gives the "size" of the unit you're buying. For example, cost of buying Network TV-E Morning is now set at the default Ad Type (:30 seconds). Leave all Ad Types set at the default.

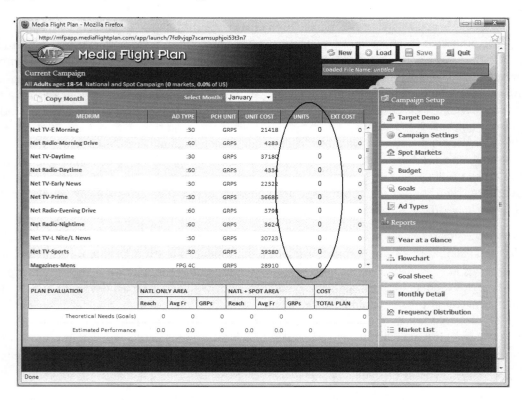

At the bottom of the screen, there is a line labeled Estimated Performance. It's in the **PLAN EVALUATION** section at the bottom of the screen. This is the only line you'll be working with – your answers will appear below the heading **NATIONAL ONLY AREA**.

Experiment 1

With your cursor in the Units column, move to Net TV-Prime and buy 50 GRPs (type 50 in the UNITS column). Observe the Estimated Performance line (bottom of screen) and write your Reach and Frequency in the first line of the table below.

Net TV-Prime	Reach	Avg Fr
50 GRPs		
100 GRPs		

Now double the GRPs – from 50 to 100 – and write your results in the table above.

A) Using the results from above, does Reach x Frequency = GRPS? (After allowance for rounding) Show the math.

B) Do 100 GRPs equal 100 percent reach? Why not? What does 100 GRPs equal?

C) Did doubling the GRPs double the reach? Why? Tip: Take a look at the sample "reach curve" below.

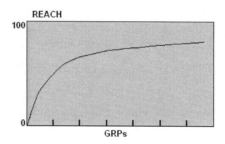

Experiment 2

In the previous experiment, we saw that 100 GRPs in Prime network television resulted in a reach of 45.5 and an average frequency of 2.2. Change the GRPs for Net TV-Prime back to 0. Now scroll down to Net Radio-Morning Drive and type in 100 GRPs. Observe results in the Estimated Performance line, and write down the new reach and frequency in the table below.

100 GRPs	Reach	Avg Fr
Net TV-Prime	45.5	2.2
Net Radio-Morning Drive		

A) Radio and TV perform very differently. After eliminating the TV buy and putting 100 GRPs into radio, Reach/Frequency changed dramatically. Why? What kind of dynamic is going on here? What's the relationship between the Reach/Frequency in radio compared to TV?

Exercise 3

B) If you were to put the same 100 GRPs into a medium that resulted in a 28 reach, what would be the average frequency? (Show the math – remember frequency is rounded to one decimal place).

What if you had a 54 reach?

Experiment 3

Comparing television cultures of different generations, which do you think watches more TV, your generation or your parents/grandparents?

We'll test your hypothesis, but first you'll need to change all the GRPs in Media Flight Plan back to 0. Now click the **Target Demo** button and change the target to Adult 18-24 (Un-check all boxes except 18-24, and click [OK]. Click [OK] in the **Target Demographic Updated** dialog box again.

Buy 100 GRPs in Network TV-Prime and write the new Reach in the table below.

Now test the older generation. Go back into **Target Demo**, uncheck the 18-24 box and check 55-64 and 65+. Write the Reach below and observe the difference.

100 GRPs	Reach
Adults 18-24	
Adults 55+	

Did your hypothesis hold?

MEDIA FLIGHT PLAN
FIAT 500 TUTORIAL

If you haven't registered yet, follow these instructions:

1. Get your *MFP* Access Code – it's located on the inside front cover of this book. Carefully scratch off the gold coating with the edge of a coin.

2. Open your internet browser.

3. Go to: **www.mediaflightplan.com**

4. Click **[New User Registration]** just under **Log in**.

5. Follow registration instructions. You'll need your access code to complete registration.

Download the tutorial

1. Log in: www.mediaflightplan.com

2. Type your email address and password, then click **[Log in]**

3. Click on **Students** at the top of the screen.

4. Click on **Ground School**. Find **'Fiat 500 Tutorial'** on the left side of the screen. Download or print the Fiat 500 Tutorial from the right side.

5. You will also want to download or print the instructions for loading and saving files. These are under the heading **'File Load and Save Instructions'**. Directions for different browsers and operating systems will be on the right.

Why is the MFP Tutorial online?

To keep *MFP* software current, our media cost database needs to remain flexible. For example, media costs change significantly each year, and posting the Tutorial online gives us the flexibility to upgrade data more frequently.

COST-PER-THOUSAND AND COST-PER-POINT

Learning Objective

Cost-Per-Thousand (CPM) and Cost-Per-Point (CPP) are basic media evaluation tools. Both democratize media choices by putting all buys on an equal footing—much like calculating cost-per-ounce when comparing Tide with Cheer at your local Super Target. After deciding which laundry brands are worth considering (or media packages in this case), you compare them for value. CPM and CPP let you compare costs even when media is delivered in different packages, e.g., full-page versus half-page, or TV versus print. Both methods let you "weigh" the cost of each medium based on a common denominator--impressions or rating points.

Cost-Per-Thousand

The "M" in CPM originates from the Roman numeral "M" for 1,000. Sometimes expressed "CPM GI," the GI is short for **G**ross **I**mpressions. Besides using gross impressions, CPM can be calculated using other data such as circulation. This would normally be done only if audience is not available - for example, in the case of an unmeasured magazine. The occasional exception aside, CPM almost always refers to gross impressions unless otherwise identified. CPMs can be compared directly, since all CPMs are calculated using the same mathematical base—the cost of delivering 1000 gross impressions to a target audience. The most common formula for CPM is:

$$CPM = \frac{total\ cost}{total\ impressions} \times 1000$$

> **Note that CPMs should be reported in dollars & cents.**

Calculating CPM for a Single Vehicle

Example Problem: Your client, Volvic brand water, (a natural, volcanic spring water imported from Europe) is targeted to younger women aged 18-39. The cost for a full-page four-color ad in *Shape* magazine is $106,045. The research department has given you a crosstab where you find that *Shape* reaches 4437 (000) women aged 18-39. What is the CPM?

> **Solving for CPM:**
>
> Cost of 4-Color page in *Shape*: $106,045
>
> Impressions converted to complete numbers: 4,437 X 1000 = 4,437,000
>
> $$\frac{\$106,045}{4,437,000} \times 1000 = \$23.90$$

Cost Per Thousand for Multiple Vehicles (Schedule CPM)

Calculating the CPM for a schedule or media plan is done by summing the gross impressions from all the insertions in all the media vehicles and dividing it into the summed cost for all the ads in the schedule.

The formula is the same as for a single ad. Assume *Vogue* has a full-page four-color cost of $100,140 and reaches 6911 (000) women 18-49. Let's look at a schedule with 2 insertions in *Vogue* along with 1 insertion in *Shape*. This buy results in the following CPM:

$$\frac{[2 \text{ (Vogue cost \$100,140)} + \text{Shape cost \$106,045]}}{[2 \text{ (Vogue Impressions 6,911,000)} + \text{Shape Impressions 4,437,000]}} \times 1000 = CPM$$

$$\frac{\$306, 325}{18,259,000} \times 1000 = \$16.78$$

Cost Per Point (CPP)
CPP does essentially the same thing as CPM – it measures efficiency. Similar to CPM, the formula is:

$$CPP = \frac{\text{Total Cost}}{\text{Total GRPs}}$$

The process for calculating the CPP for a schedule is the same—obtain the total cost by summing the cost of all the adds, and divide by the total GRPs obtained by summing the ratings of all the adds. CPP is usually rounded to the nearest whole dollar.

CPM typically used for print media — CPP preferred for broadcast media
When comparing media options, CPMs and CPPs perform the same function. Each tool makes it possible to see which vehicle or schedule is most cost efficient despite each media plan having a different mix of media, ad sizes or other elements. **Your decision will be the same regardless of which tool you use— the schedule with the lowest CPM will always have the lowest CPP as well**. Ultimately it's a matter of preference, although because of the way syndicated data are reported and used, print is typically compared using cost-per-thousand, while broadcast tends to be compared using cost-per-point.

When planners are in the early stages using rough cost estimates, most use a 'typical cost-per-point' supplied by the broadcast buying group. Because numerous spots are purchased, it's easier to work with CPPs in broadcast to estimate how many Gross Rating Points can be purchased with a given budget.

Efficiency is the rule, but every rule . . .
When one vehicle or plan reaches the target at a lower cost than another, we say it is "more efficient." Efficiency, however, is not always the best strategy. When Saturn launched their new brand, Hal Riney and Partners made a bold print buy. Their media strategy — "full speed ahead and damn the CPMs". They targeted women 18-34 by purchasing magazines that *enjoyed at least 30 minutes reading time*. CPMs took a back seat based on the strategy that quality reading time trumps efficiency.

Calculating Cost Per Point (CPP)
Example Problem: Continuing with *Shape* and *Vogue*, the research tabulation shows that for women 18-49, the ratings for the two magazines are 6.7 and 10.4 respectively. Which has the lowest Cost Per Point? What is the CPP of a schedule consisting of 3 full-page four color insertions in *Vogue* and 4 in *Shape* each publication?

Solving for CPP: First, calculate the CPP for each publication, using the CPP formula:

$$\text{CPP for Shape} = \frac{\$106,045}{6.7} = \$15,828 \ (\$15,827.61 \text{ rounded})$$

$$\text{CPP for Vogue} = \frac{\$100,140}{10.4} = \$9,629 \ (\$9,628.85 \text{ rounded})$$

For this target, *Vogue* is more efficient (the CPP is $6,000+ lower). As already noted, you may not always use the most efficient cost—editorial environment or value-added packages often trump CPP.

To get the cost of three insertions, calculate total cost and total gross rating points, then use the formula:

$$\frac{[3\ (Vogue\ \text{cost}\ \$100{,}140) + 4\ (Shape\ \text{cost}\ \$106{,}045)]}{[3\ (Vogue\ \text{rating}\ 10.4) + 4\ (Shape\ \text{rating}\ 6.7)]} = CPP$$

$$\frac{\$724{,}600}{58.0\ GRPS} = \$1{,}249\ (\$1{,}249.31\ \text{rounded})$$

Problems

1. Calculate **CPM, Total Cost,** and **Total Gross Impressions** for each of the magazine titles shown in the table below. As you do the math, FILL IN ALL OF THE EMPTY CELLS. You may wish to use a spreadsheet like Microsoft Excel.

Publication	Full-Page 4-Color Cost	Women Aud (000)	CPM	Schedule Insertions	Total Cost	Total Gross Imp (000)
Parenting	$125,765	9,216		3		
Parent's	129,200	11,633		6		
Prevention	11,300	8,392		2		
Reader's Digest	234,900	23,234		4		
Redbook	121,500	8,537		2		
Time	223,000	11,023		5		
TV Guide	166,100	15,963		2		
Woman's Day	214,750	19,364		3		
Vogue	94,470	8,500		3		
Schedule Totals	----	----		30		

2. Which of the magazines in Exhibit I is the most efficient – has the lowest CPM? Name the magazine and show your math for calculating the CPM.

3. Which has the highest CPM (is *least* efficient) among all magazines on the list? Name the magazine and show your math for calculating CPM.

4. The universe for women is 106,894 (000). What is the rating for *Redbook* and *Woman's Day*? If you've forgotten how to calculate ratings, review the formulas in Exercises 1 & 2. Show your math.

5. Using the information supplied in the following table, fill in the missing values for ALL EMPTY CELLS. Remember to round CPP to the nearest dollar.

Program	:30 Cost	HH Rating	CPP	Schedule Insertions	Total Cost	GRPs
The Mentalist	$330,000	16.9		1		
Sunday Movie	124,200	8.4		2		
Survivor	245,800	11.5		1		
20/20	115,600	6.2		3		
60 Minutes	89,100	8.7		2		
Schedule Totals	----	----		9		

6. What is the **CPP** for *Survivor*? What does it mean?

7. Relating to the TV programs above, Nielsen Media Research estimates that Total TV Homes for the season is 109.6 MM. How many impressions are produced by **one** ad in *20/20*? (If you've forgotten, find the formula in the *Gross Rating Points, Reach & Frequency* exercise that solves for impressions.)

8. What is a Gross Rating Point? Using the universe in question 7, how many impressions are in one **GRP**?

USING SYNDICATED CONSUMER RESEARCH

Learning Objective
Marketers and agencies use a variety of research to help them understand consumers. One of the principal tools is syndicated research; it gathers comprehensive data from thousands of consumers to help marketers make intelligent, informed decisions. These large studies are done by independent companies and sold to many different clients, including ad agencies and corporations. Generally speaking, syndicated market researchers collect data about magazine readership (often the principal reason for the study), consumer attitudes and purchase behavior, and other media usage. Thousands of data points are collected from individual consumers via personal interviews, phone interviews, and product usage questionnaires.

Syndicated Research
Mediamark Research Inc (MRI) and Simmons are among the major providers of general consumer studies. Other consumer research may be available at many ad agencies depending on client needs. Examples include studies on vehicle owners done by JD Power and Associates, Monroe Mendelsohn's study of the affluent, and MARS, a study for the pharmaceutical industry.

The data compiled by different research companies is distributed through various crosstabbing systems. As a marketer you need to know how to interpret these data formats and tabbing systems – often quite similar among various syndicated providers. This exercise will help you learn to read and understand the tabulations generated by these systems.

How to Interpret Crosstabs
Find **Exhibit I** (after the problems at the end of this exercise) – it shows part of a typical crosstab format. At the very top of the tab, the base is identified as **Adults**. The base of a crosstab can be whatever you wish, but it is the universe within which the tabulation is done. The first row of data and the first column are labeled **Totals**. This row and column contains the total number of base persons in each row or column category. The first cell in the first row, where the two "Totals" intersect, shows the total number of persons contained in the base, and the associated percentages that go with it:

		Totals
Totals	(000)	209373
	Vert%	100.0
	Horz%	100.0
	Index	100

Why is the Data Weighted?
This cell shows that there are **209,373,000** adults in the US. The number in the row labeled **(000)** is called the projection, or count. It's the estimated number of persons in the cell. The reason it's called a "projection" is that the respondents in the cell are reported as "projected" to the universe they represent using weights. Research companies estimate the value of each respondent, then sum the weights of each actual respondent to 'project' the sample up to the universe the cell represents. The vertical and horizontal percentages are 100.0% in this case because the total is everyone in the universe. Indexes represent concentration or potential, and will be discussed in depth in the next exercise.

Although not shown in this example, some tabulations will show the number of respondents in a line that is labeled **UNWTD** (for unweighted). It's tempting to think that there is a linear relationship between the two—but there is not. Each respondent has a different weight, depending on his/her characteristics. Therefore, the two rows are NOT interchangeable in representing the universe. If both Unwgt and (000) are shown, be sure to use the correct row: **(000)**.

Read Rows Horizontally – Read Columns Vertically

Each cell follows the same format—the first number in the block is the raw number of persons who meet the requirements of both the row and the column. Look at the cell (in Exhibit I) where **Men** intersects **Attended Movies Past 6 Months**. You are in the right place if the number on the (000) row is **59851**. The cell should be read, "**59,851,000 men attended a movie in the past 6 months**". Move your finger to the top number in this same column (the "Totals" row). There you will find the **Total** number of persons who went to a movie in the past 6 months: **128,136,000** (remember the numbers in this tab are shown in thousands– mentally add 3 zeros).

The **Vert%** shows that **46.7** percent of adults who went to a movie in the past 6 months were men. You know to use the vertical percentage because the two numbers are **vertically opposed** (one above the other) in the same column. The math is straightforward: **59,851 ÷ 128,136 x 100 = 46.7 percent**.

Move back to the previous cell. Looking across to the totals column on the left, note that total MEN in the survey = **100,457** (000). Because the two cells are **horizontally** opposed in the same row, the horizontal percent represents the ratio of men who attended a movie in the past 6 months as a percent of TOTAL men: **59,851 ÷ 100,457 X 100 = 59.6**, the percentage shown.

Totals are Denominators

The **total** for any column or row is always the **denominator**. Obviously, the other half of the equation must be the numerator – the number in any cell is always the numerator in the ratio. (For examples, see the equations shown at bottom of the **Horiz%** and **Vert%** boxes in Exhibit I). Percentages are extremely helpful and can save a lot of work if you make sure you know which ones to use.

Now find the row **8+ CHILDREN IN HH** and the column labeled **Attend Movies 2x/Month or more**. The cell where they intersect has an asterisk (*) next to it. Look at the bottom of the tab sheet; there's a footnote indicating that this cell has insufficient sample size to reliably project, and that caution should be used in interpreting the data. The cutoff for flagging data is different for each data source, but is typically around 50 respondents. If your crosstab has a lot of asterisks, it is an indication that the columns are too narrowly defined, and you should consider making the group larger, even if it doesn't define the target as precisely as you'd like. It's better to have good data for a reasonable likeness of your desired target than to have useless data for exactly what you want.

The last label in each row's data set is **Index**. (Find the **Index** box). For now it is sufficient to know that they indicate the likelihood or potential of an activity or characteristic in the cell. A 100 Index indicates the "average", and indexes above 100 indicate greater than average propensity, while indexes below 100 indicate below average – less likelihood that a behavior or condition exists.

Crosstabs can be quite lengthy; it's not unusual to run tabs many columns across and up to hundreds of pages long. For example, MRI, Simmons, and others query respondents on hundreds of product categories, and several thousands of brands within those categories. Audiences are collected for well over 200 magazines, and many network and syndicated television programs, cable networks, newspapers, radio and other items!

Problems

Data needed for these problems is available online: www.mediaflightplan.com
You can look at the data on-screen, or download it and print. It's an Excel file about 10 pages long, and will be used for the next exercise, so hold on to it if you print it out.

If you haven't downloaded it yet, go to **mediaflightplan.com** and click on **Student**. Next, click **Ground School**. Then, click on the link to download MRI data. It's titled: *MRI Movie Cross Tab Data*

VERY IMPORTANT TIP: Is it a Horizontal or Vertical problem? First look for the two projections (raw base numbers) referred to in the problem. If the two base numbers are horizontally opposed, it is a horizontal problem, and the percentage you need is in the row labeled HORZ%. If the two projections (raw base numbers) are vertically opposed – one above the other – it is a vertical problem, and the percentage you need is in the row labeled VERT%. Always find both raw numbers first, then divide to make sure you've got the right percentage.

NOTE: Round all of your percentages to one place – e.g., 24.07 = 24.1

1. How many **Adults** say they **Attended Movies Past 6 Months**? (See page 1 of MRI data). Tip: This tab shows **Unwgt** respondents; use the projection row labeled **(000)**.

2. Referring back to question number 1, all of the projections in this cross tab are displayed in a common, numerical way. All projections are expressed numerically in _____.

3. Among all Adults who GRADUATED HIGH SCHOOL, what percent **Prefer to See Movie On Opening Weekend**? (We're still on pg. 1) Is this a horizontal or vertical problem? Show math used to get the percentage. Tip: Break each problem into bite-size units, and *always begin by finding the two base numbers*. In this problem, first find the projected number of Adults who GRADUATED HIGH SCHOOL in the **Totals** column. Start at top of the **Totals** column and follow it *down* to the projection row (000). Next, follow this row *across* and find the projected number who **Prefer to See Movie On Opening Weekend**. Last, divide the two numbers, and then multiply by 100 to verify that you have the correct percentage. (Note that it's reported as either **Vert%** or **Horz%**; your job is to decide which is correct.) Show complete equation below:

4. Targeting adults who **Attend Movies Once a Month,** list the seven marketing regions. Start with PACIFIC— MKTG REGN on Page 8 and follow through on page 9. Rank these seven markets from high to low based on the *percentage* of adults who **Attend Movies Once a Month** in each geographic region. Is this a vertical or horizontal problem? Tip: Begin by calculating the PACIFIC-MKTG REGN. The numerator for this equation is found on pg. 8 in the **Attend Movies Once a Month** column. The denominator for all seven markets is in the projected **Totals** row on page 1. Be sure to use the correct total – the projected total below the column **Attend Movies Once a Month**. List all seven markets, show the equation for each, and rank them 1-7.

Exercise 6

5. Of all **Adults** with CHILDREN 6-11 YEARS, what percent **Prefer to See Movie On Opening Weekend**? Is this horizontal or vertical? Show the math.

6. Among adults who **Prefer to See Movie on Opening Weekend,** what percent have CHILDREN 6-11 YEARS? Horizontal or vertical? Show your math.

7. Find the set of data for WORKING WOMEN. Among the three groups listed below, which has the highest percentage of movie goers that are WORKING WOMEN? Tip: Although focusing on working women, you still need to consider them as part of the total number of movie goers.

- **Prefer to See Movie On Opening Weekend**
- **Prefer to See Within 1st 2 Wks After Open Wknd**
- **Prefer to See After Second Week**

Is this a Horizontal or Vertical problem? Show Math.

8. Of all MEN who **Attended Movies Past 6 Months**, what percentage **Prefer to See Movie On Opening Weekend**? Tip: This is a bit of a brainteaser because the percentage (**Vert%** or **Horz%**) is **NOT** reported for you on the tab.

EXHIBIT I

Note: Exhibit I corresponds with the first two pages of this exercise. It may be easier to follow along if you tear this sheet out.

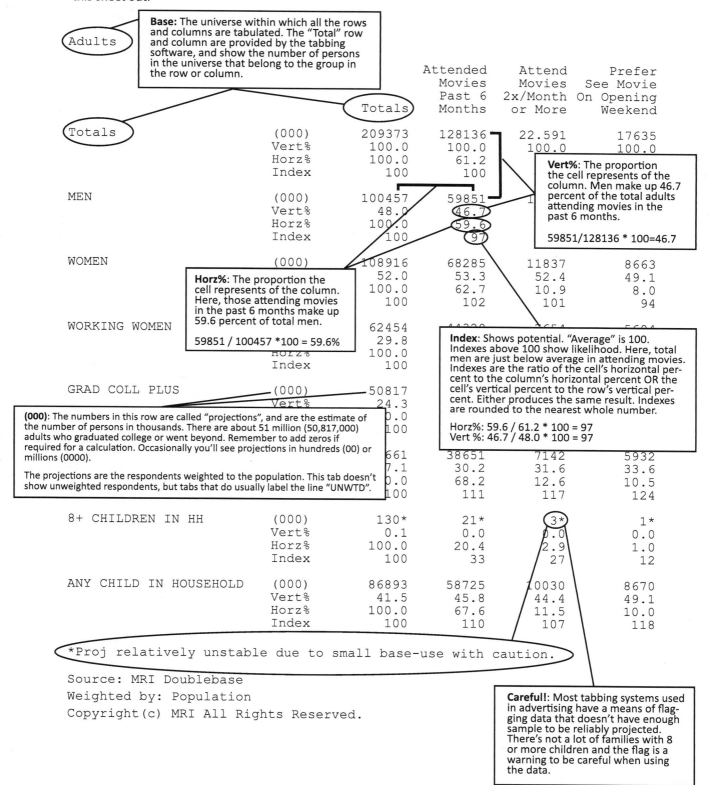

Adults

Base: The universe within which all the rows and columns are tabulated. The "Total" row and column are provided by the tabbing software, and show the number of persons in the universe that belong to the group in the row or column.

		Attended Movies Past 6 Months	Attend Movies 2x/Month or More	Prefer See Movie On Opening Weekend
Totals	(000)	209373	128136	22.591	17635
	Vert%	100.0	100.0	100.0	100.0
	Horz%	100.0	61.2		
	Index	100	100		
MEN	(000)	100457	59851	1	
	Vert%	48.0	46.7		
	Horz%	100.0	59.6		
	Index	100	97		
WOMEN	(000)	108916	68285	11837	8663
	Vert%	52.0	53.3	52.4	49.1
	Horz%	100.0	62.7	10.9	8.0
	Index	100	102	101	94
WORKING WOMEN	(000)	62454	44300	7654	5694
	Vert%	29.8			
	Horz%	100.0			
	Index	100			
GRAD COLL PLUS	(000)	50817	38651	7142	5932
	Vert%	24.3	30.2	31.6	33.6
	Horz%	100.0	68.2	12.6	10.5
	Index	100	111	117	124
8+ CHILDREN IN HH	(000)	130*	21*	3*	1*
	Vert%	0.1	0.0	0.0	0.0
	Horz%	100.0	20.4	2.9	1.0
	Index	100	33	27	12
ANY CHILD IN HOUSEHOLD	(000)	86893	58725	10030	8670
	Vert%	41.5	45.8	44.4	49.1
	Horz%	100.0	67.6	11.5	10.0
	Index	100	110	107	118

Vert%: The proportion the cell represents of the column. Men make up 46.7 percent of the total adults attending movies in the past 6 months.

59851/128136 * 100=46.7

Horz%: The proportion the cell represents of the column. Here, those attending movies in the past 6 months make up 59.6 percent of total men.

59851 / 100457 *100 = 59.6%

Index: Shows potential. "Average" is 100. Indexes above 100 show likelihood. Here, total men are just below average in attending movies. Indexes are the ratio of the cell's horizontal percent to the column's horizontal percent OR the cell's vertical percent to the row's vertical percent. Either produces the same result. Indexes are rounded to the nearest whole number.

Horz%: 59.6 / 61.2 * 100 = 97
Vert %: 46.7 / 48.0 * 100 = 97

(000): The numbers in this row are called "projections", and are the estimate of the number of persons in thousands. There are about 51 million (50,817,000) adults who graduated college or went beyond. Remember to add zeros if required for a calculation. Occasionally you'll see projections in hundreds (00) or millions (0000).

The projections are the respondents weighted to the population. This tab doesn't show unweighted respondents, but tabs that do usually label the line "UNWTD".

*Proj relatively unstable due to small base-use with caution.

Source: MRI Doublebase
Weighted by: Population
Copyright(c) MRI All Rights Reserved.

Careful!: Most tabbing systems used in advertising have a means of flagging data that doesn't have enough sample to be reliably projected. There's not a lot of families with 8 or more children and the flag is a warning to be careful when using the data.

USING INDEXES TO IDENTIFY TARGET AUDIENCES

Learning Objective

Learn to calculate and understand fundamental usage of index numbers. Index numbers allow planners to compare potential for usage of a product/brand across demographic groups or across media users.

Offensive and Defensive Marketing Strategies

A defensive marketing posture protects the marketing franchise that a brand has already built up. Often the best strategic decision is to spend media dollars wherever current sales are highest. In contrast, an offensive approach is one of conquest where you would spend in markets where your brand has the highest potential, not necessarily highest sales. Both offense and defense have their place in marketing strategy, and one is not necessarily better than the other. Indices help marketers see areas of strength and weakness.

Indexes

An index compares a product's usage within a demographic group relative to usage within the total population. It helps marketers to discover whether a particular demographic group is more or less likely to consume a product/brand compared to the total population. For example, if professional/managerial people are much more likely to buy imported cars, index numbers would be significantly higher for this group. If you were a brand manager for BMW, you might concentrate media pressure on a professional/managerial target because of their higher potential for purchasing a BMW.

Index numbers provide a way of putting two different numbers on the same "base" or "scale" so that they can be compared easily. In crosstabs, indexes are usually of composition that corresponds to vertical percents. For example, if we only had the vertical percents in EXHIBIT I, we might assume that the 12.8% shown for HEAVY USERS OF PACKAGED DINNERS Age 45-54 is better than the 10.1% shown for Age 18-24. That's because we don't have these percentages in context, compared to the groups from which they come. If we take those percents and compare them to the corresponding proportions in the population we would find that the 10.1 vertical percent for Age 18-24 represents a higher concentration of heavy users. And, that is exactly how indexes are calculated.

Calculating Indexes

To compute the index for Age 18-24, divide the proportion that Age 18-24 represents among HEAVY USERS by the proportion that Age 18-24 represents in the population, and multiply by 100. *Index numbers are always rounded to the nearest whole number.*

$$index = \frac{\% \text{ demo in target group}}{\% \text{ demo in base population}} \times 100$$

Age 18-24 Heavy User of Packaged Dinners Index: 10.1 ÷ 8.8 X 100 = 115 Index
Age 45-54 Heavy User of Packaged Dinners Index: 12.8 ÷ 15.3 X 100 = 84 Index

Index numbers are constructed so that *100* represents the average potential for usage—in other words, the proportion of usage for a group is exactly the same as its proportion of the population. An index greater than 100 is above average, and an index below 100 represents a group with lower than average potential. In this example, if you were to "grab a handful" of 18-24 year olds, you'd be 15 percent (115 Index) *more likely* than average to find a heavy user of packaged dinners than if you grabbed a handful of the population. Conversely, you'd be 16 percent *less likely* (see 84 Index) to find a heavy user among 45-54 year olds (100-

84=16).

While we've shown how one way indexes are calculated to provide some understanding, the focus of this exercise is *using* indexes. More discussion on different kinds of indexes comes in a later exercise.

Using Indexes

While comparing demographic groups, you should initially highlight groups with index numbers over 100. Think of high index numbers as "flags." They save time by identifying important demographic factors, but high index numbers are not to be trusted without careful scrutiny. Low indexes are also important because they tend to show activities or products that are less popular among the target group. Index numbers are helpful, but do not reveal the whole picture. Planners must take care to use them intelligently. *Never trust an index number until you have examined the projections (the "000" row) for all the demos in a group*.

Look at the set of age groupings in EXHIBIT I. Among all age groups who are HEAVY USERS OF PACKAGED DINNERS, 128 is the highest index number. If you selected your target audience based on this index alone, you would choose the 35-44 age group. However, the younger 25-34 age group also offers high sales potential, with an index of 124. Despite a slightly lower index, this group is still well above average, and represents nearly a third of all heavy users (Vert%=29.5). Reasoning: Age 25-34 is actually bigger (2.3 million bigger) than Age 35-44, and includes more heavy users (251,000 more). Despite the lower index number for Age 25-34 (4 points lower), it would be smart to combine both groups into one target audience.

Whenever the spread between index numbers in a grouping is not significant (10 points or less), it often makes sense to combine or collapse the groups into a single target audience.

EXHIBIT I

		Total Shoppers	Hvy Users Pkgd Dinners
Totals(000)	112018	15518	
	Vert%	100.0	100.0
	Horz%	100.0	13.9
	Index	100	100
Age 18-24	(000)	9907	1559
	Vert%	8.8	10.1
	Horz%	100.0	15.7
	Index	100	115
Age 25-34	(000)	26761	4585
	Vert%	23.9	29.5
	Horz%	100.0	17.1
	Index	100	124
Age 35-44	(000)	24489	4334
	Vert%	21.9	27.9
	Horz%	100.0	17.8
	Index	100	128
Age 45-54	(000)	17156	1990
	Vert%	15.3	12.8
	Horz%	100.0	11.6
	Index	100	84
Age 55+	(000)	33706	3050
	Vert%	30.1	19.7
	Horz%	100	9.0
	Index	100	65

Begin by highlighting all demo groups with index numbers greater than 100. Next, within a demo set, if adjoining demos are significantly above average, combine them into a single target if they are a good "fit."

Problems

If an index is above 100 and higher than other indexes in the same group (age, income, etc.) by 10 points or more, use the index as the initial criterion for target selection. However, if the spread between the index numbers is less than 10 points, consider the size of each group (the projection (000) or vertical percent) as the best way to pick the winner. Also keep in mind that index numbers somewhat below 100 should not be ignored if the projections are promising. It is common to include multiple target demos in a media strategy, but still give priority a group representing a significant proportion of the population when the spread between the indices is not significant. *Be sure to use the projections, not the UNWTD counts when doing the problems.*

If you haven't downloaded it yet, go to **mediaflightplan.com** and click on **MFP Ground School**. Then click on the link to download MRI data: *MRI Movie Cross Tab Data*

1. Assume your target is **Adults** who **Prefer to See Movie on Opening Weekend**. Based solely on index numbers, which AGE group has greater potential? (See AGE groups in MRI data pg. 2)

2. As noted, *it often makes sense to combine or collapse multiple target groups into a single target audience.* Continuing with **Adults** who **Prefer to See Movie on Opening Weekend,** which is the "next best" demo group that makes the most sense to combine with the demo you selected in question 1?

    a) Cite both index numbers.
    b) What is the new projected **Total (000)** users who would be in this combined target audience?

3. Stay with **Prefer to See Movie On Opening Weekend,** and evaluate occupation as a demo set – set begins with demos titled: NON EMPLOYED, PROFESSIONAL/MANAGERIAL, etc.

    a) Based on index numbers alone for all five occupations, *name the two occupation demo groups* offering the greatest potential and list their index numbers.
    b) A third demo group could be included, even though it has a lower index. Which one? Explain why.

4. Go to the page with a set of **HHI index numbers**. In the column **Attended Movies Past 6 Months**, highlight all eight of the index numbers.

a) Plot the indexes and draw a line through them to make a line chart below. Analyze the trend you see.

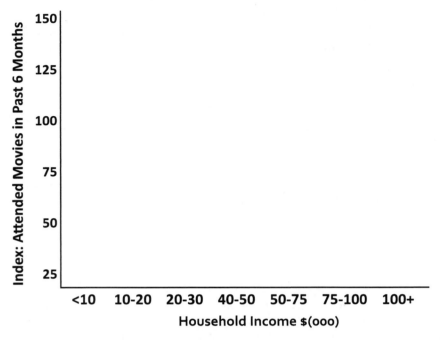

b) Speculate on *why* this pattern exists – give several reasons why this pattern emerges. Check MRI for relevance of education and income, and cite the data in your answer.

5. Your client, the owner a national Drive-In movie chain, has noticed resurgence in attendance and she wants to expand into new locations. Knowing she cannot compete with the multiplex cinemas in the metro cities, she is conducting marketing analysis in rural areas – known locations where drive-ins are still popular. MRI provides three levels of movie attendance: **Attend Movies 2x Month or More, Attend Movies Once a Month,** and **Attend Movies Less than 1x/Month.** You have this data for COUNTY SIZE C and COUNTY SIZE D – both more rural and farming areas. Though both C and D counties contain roughly the same population, your client needs to know if there is any significant difference in attendance and if she should focus on one or the other. Use the population projections (000) together with attendance groups (see box below) to calculate the monthly gross movie attendance for C and D counties:

Attendance Group   **Weight**

2 x A Month or More 3

Once a Month 1

Less Than Once A Month 0.5

The concept of "weighting" is covered in depth the exercise *Factor"Spreadsheeting" With a Pocket Calculator.* For now, consider "weighting" a tool used to assign added value to target groups, target markets and other marketing variables. Here, the marketer has decided that 2 x A Month movie goers are 3 times more valuable than once a month movie goers. Weighting allows the marketer to manipulate the value of both counties based on movie attendance.

Follow these seven steps to weight the attendance groups and calculate the index.

(1) Consult the MRI data for COUNTY SIZE C and COUNTY SIZE D projections based on *Attendance Groups* shown in the table below.

(2) Write these Projections (000) into the corresponding cells in the table below.

3) Multiply Est.Weight x Proj (000) to get Gross Movies for each county size.

4) Sum each of the Gross Movies columns to get Total Gross Movies (000) for each county size.

5) Consulting MRI data, write the Total Adults Proj (000) for each county size. (Careful - use Total Adults, NOT Total County Size movie attenders).

6) Compute the average number of movies per person ("Per Capita Movies") for both county sizes by dividing Total Gross Movies (000) by the Total Adults Proj (000).

7) Calculate the index number to discover relative movie attendance rates based on County Size. To calculate the index, divide the "Per Capita" movie attendance for County C by the Per Capita attendance for County D, and multiply by 100. Calculating the index is NOT enough. Your client wants you to articulate what this index number means. Review calculating index numbers on the first page of this exercise to properly explain your answer.

Attendance Groups	County Size C			County Size D		
	Est. Weight	Proj (000)	Gross Movies	Est. Weight	Proj (000)	Gross Movies
2x/Month or More	3	X	=	3	X	=
Once a Month	1	X	=	1	X	=
Less Than 1x/Month	0.5	X	=	0.5	X	=
Total Gross Movies (000)			Sum			Sum
Total Adults Proj (000)						
Per Capita Movies (Total Gross Movies ÷ Total Adults Proj)						
* Index C to D Counties (C Cnty Per Capita ÷ D Cnty Per Capita X 100)						

Write **index** number (final answer) here:

*A different kind of index: This may be one of the simplest applications of indexing. Unlike the example on the first page of this exercise, here we are simply comparing two types of movie goers based on projected attendance. It's an index number based on a ratio of two market behaviors in two geographic locations, county size C and county size D.

CATEGORY AND BRAND DEVELOPMENT INDEXES BDI & CDI

Learning Objective
Category and brand development indexes can help you decide if a market deserves extra advertising/marketing dollars or any dollars at all. You'll also learn how to calculate both indexes and get a basic understanding of what they mean and how they can be used.

Background on CDI/BDI Usage
Often planners have to make decisions about placement of additional advertising weight in a market. While the index numbers in the syndicated data might inform you about the relative importance of different regions with respect to the potential for usage of the product/brand, these regional breakdowns are very broad in scope. Clients often have sales data for individual markets. When available, planners prefer using objective, market specific data. This is where the Category Development Index (CDI) and the Brand Development Index (BDI) are used.

The CDI and BDI compare the sales of a product category or a brand with the potential for sales of that category or brand based on the population in each market. If a market accounted for two percent of the U.S. population, the assumption is that it should account for two percent of the product or brand's sales. This would reflect an average level of consumption and would be seen in an index of 100, the average. In reality, markets account for varying levels of sales that often are not in direct proportion to the population that market represents. The CDI and BDI identify specific markets that account for heavy usage of a product/brand, and if the advertiser intends to target the campaign toward the heavy user, these index numbers help identify those markets for the advertiser. BDI and CDI can also be used to identify areas of opportunity or weakness which a marketer may want or need to address.

Calculating Development Indexes
BDI and CDI can be calculated for any geographic area, although you will probably see media markets most frequently. Sometimes clients cannot provide the data on a media market basis, and you will have to use your best judgment in applying county or state level data to the specific situation. While BDI and CDI are generally calculated using sales or revenue, other items may occasionally be used as surrogates, such as store count or vehicle registrations. The CDI is calculated like this:

$$\text{Category Development Index (CDI)} = \frac{\text{\% of category sales in area}}{\text{\% of population in area}} \times 100$$

Calculation of Brand Development Index is identical, except that brand sales are substituted for category sales:

$$\text{Brand Development Index (BDI)} = \frac{\text{\% of brand sales in area}}{\text{\% of population in area}} \times 100$$

By convention, both CDI and BDI are rounded to whole numbers.

Jacuzzi spa Example: 5.25% of all sales of whirlpool spas take place in the Los Angeles metro market, and your company, Jacuzzi, sells 6.0% of its product in the LA market. If the Los Angeles metro has 4.2% of U.S. population, calculate the category and brand development indexes and explain what they mean.

Calculating CDI and BDI for Jacuzzi:

$$CDI = \frac{\% \text{ of category sales in area}}{\% \text{ of population in area}} \times 100 = \frac{5.25}{4.2} \times 100 = 125$$

$$BDI = \frac{\% \text{ of brand sales in area}}{\% \text{ of population in area}} \times 100 = \frac{6.0}{4.2} \times 100 = 143 \text{ (142.8 rounded)}$$

The Los Angeles metro is a great market for whirlpool spas—both the category (CDI) and brand (BDI) development indexes are greater than 100, indicating above average sales for the category and especially for the Jacuzzi brand.

Using CDI and BDI to evaluate markets

CDI and BDI should not be the only marketing data used in making a media decision. However, if we assume all other marketing criteria are equal, then CDI and BDI would likely take on added importance. The relative weight that is given to the CDI or BDI varies, depending on the situation. Sometimes a marketer may choose to give added weight to CDI over BDI; at other times the reverse might hold true. One way of assessing markets is to compare the BDI and CDI based on one of the following four scenarios:

> **Scenario 1. High CDI and High BDI**
>
> **Scenario 2. High CDI and Low BDI**
>
> **Scenario 3. Low CDI and High BDI**
>
> **Scenario 4. Low CDI and Low BDI**

Scenario 1 represents a market where both the category and the brand are doing very well and, therefore, is a promising market. Often these markets are singled out for added media emphasis.

Scenario 2 is a market where the brand is doing poorly compared to the category. This market might be seen as one where there is room for the brand to grow. However, some research must be done to find out the reasons for the poor showing of the brand and subsequently, marketing or advertising must address the problem.

Scenario 3 is a market where even though the brand is doing well, the product category is showing lower potential. This is a situation where reasons for the poor showing of the category must be investigated. If the category has been showing continuous decline, then it might not be worth the added investment to advertise the brand even though it might be doing well. However, if a category will remain constant or can be rejuvenated, then advertising for the brand may well be worth the investment. The advertising message might need to encourage product category usage rather than brand usage exclusively.

Scenario 4 on first glance is a no-win situation. When both the product category and brand are languishing, additional advertising investment must be based on compelling reasons.

CDI and BDI are only one set of criteria that are used in making decisions about which markets deserve additional advertising weight. The strength of index numbers is that they are based on sales data and are, therefore, objective data. It makes sense for a marketer to concentrate media pressure in markets where brands are already doing well or are likely to do well because the product category shows promise.

Problems

1. If San Francisco accounts for 1.24 percent of total U.S. population, and has 1.43 percent of total U.S. laundry detergent sales, what is the CDI for this market? Also, what does this index mean? **The convention for CDIs and BDIs is to express them as whole numbers**. Use the formulas shown at the beginning of this exercise, and show your math below.

2. You are marketing Red Baron frozen pizza, and you are looking for some place to spend $50,000 in surplus advertising budget. You have narrowed the choice down to two markets: Seattle and San Francisco. Calculate the BDI/CDI for both markets. If the surplus can only be spent in one market, based on BDI/CDI ONLY, which market should you choose?

Market	%US	%Red Baron	%Frozen Pizza
Seattle	0.9	1.6	1.9
San Francisco	1.7	2.8	3.0

Exercise 8

3. You are the Marketing Director for *Great Lakes'* brand *Cherry Treats*, a regional company headquartered in Traverse City, MI. You distribute cherry-based snack products made from Michigan cherries exclusively, and you sell to the markets that surround Lake Michigan. Competition comes from all other brands in the category, referred to by Great Lakes as *Fruited Snacks*.

TIPS: To simplify this problem, assume that these seven markets comprise the **total universe** for your brand. Likewise, the 6,308.5 (000) Households in the table below represent 100% of the population. The $3 million in sales for Great Lakes and the $27 million for Fruited Snacks also represent totals for the "universe".

Using data provided in the table below, calculate the BDI and CDI for each market. Begin by converting the data to percentages; then calculate the BDIs and CDIs using the formulas illustrated in the examples above.

Market	HHs (000)	%HHs	Great Lakes Sales $(000)	% Great Lakes Sales	Fruited Snack Sales $(000)	% Fruited Snack Sales	BDI	CDI
Chicago	3,449.3		1,350		14,040			
Grand Rapids	727.1		390		2,160			
Green Bay	424.2		180		1,890			
Lansing	256.2		180		1,350			
Milwaukee	872.7		450		3,510			
South Bend	332.3		150		1,890			
Traverse City	246.7		300		2,160			
TOTALS	6,308.5		3,000		27,000			

Tip for answering all of the following questions: Index numbers have value but they may fall short of a complete answer; consider other data from this table to add substance.

4. Name the markets with both high BDI and high CDI, and advise your client on the best advertising/marketing action in light of your brand, the category, and potential competitive threats.

5. Name the markets with high BDI and low CDI, and advise your client on the best advertising/marketing action in light of your brand, the category, and potential competitive threats.

6. Name the markets with low BDI and high CDI, and advise your client on the best advertising/marketing action in light of your brand, the category, and potential competitive threats.

7. Name the markets with both low BDI and low CDI, and advise your client on the best advertising/marketing action in light of your brand, the category, and potential competitive threats.

USING QUINTILES TO EVALUATE MEDIA POTENTIAL

Learning Objective

Learn to define "tiles" (quintiles, quartiles, terciles, etc.) and how they are constructed. This exercise will also show one of the ways tiles are used – to evaluate media consumption.

Background

Quintiles are a specific case of "tiling"--a technique that breaks a population into roughly equal groups to highlight differences in product or media consumption. There is nothing magic about quintiles, terciles or quartiles (other tilings are also used). They are simply a convenient way to group people. Organizing people into "quintiles" is simply dividing an ordered population into five roughly equal groups. Likewise, quartiles would be groups containing one-fourth of a population, etc.

To construct tiles, the respondent group or population is ranked from high to low on a particular characteristic, for example, "bars of soap used in the last 30 days." Then starting from the heaviest user, persons are counted off until there are sufficient to complete the first tile. In a universe of 100 persons, twenty would be placed into each quintile. If using terciles, there would be 33 in each group. The completed tile groups can be used to analyze demographic characteristics or media usage.

Application

Media quintiles can be used to determine what media affinities exist for various consumer products and categories. Note that once a person's quintile for a medium is determined, it does not change based on product usage. This makes it possible to find concentrations of heavy or light users of a medium regardless of the product beign analyzed.

In Exhibit I, the heaviest viewers of TV – in Quintile 1 – make up 20% of the population (by definition, since adults were the basis for the quintile), but 35 percent of all Gum Users are in the heaviest TV usage group. **The Heavy TV – Quintile 1 – index for Gum Users is 175 (35 ÷ 20 X 100 = 175 Index)** indicating TV is a good way to reach Gum Users because a disproportionate number of Gum Users (75% above average 100 index) are Heavy TV Users.

Twisted? Higher Index Numbers in Quintiles IV and V = Lighter Usage

In many media surveys, Quintile I represents the heaviest usage group, Quintile II next heaviest, and so forth until Quintile V, lightest usage group. **Heads up**: If a high index number shows up in Quintile IV or V for television (e.g. the index is above 100 for the low usage quintiles), it means the group is *above average for low usage* (twisted, but true)—in other words, the medium is not used as heavily. Even so, you may need to use the medium—while overall television usage may be lower, there will likely be some programs that do a good job reaching the target.

Exhibit I
Gum Users by TV Viewing Quintiles

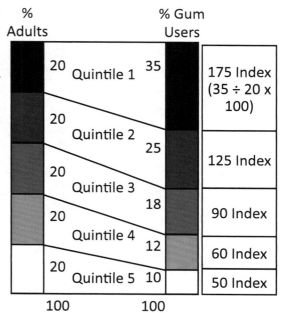

% Adults		% Gum Users	
20	Quintile 1	35	175 Index (35 ÷ 20 x 100)
20	Quintile 2	25	125 Index
20	Quintile 3	18	90 Index
20	Quintile 4	12	60 Index
20	Quintile 5	10	50 Index
100		100	

Exercise 9

When using real data, it's important to note that human beings rarely have the courtesy to form perfect, equal size groups of media usage. Most all frequency distributions have "lumps"-- cells that are unusually large in size. In theory, each quintile should contain exactly 20% of the total sample. But when using survey data, persons at a particular frequency level are often kept together, because logically they belong together (e.g., if most of the people in the "5"level would fall into the 3-5 group in a perfect split, it usually makes more sense to keep all "5" level persons together in the 3-5 group rather than splitting them up and putting part of them with a 6-10 group). Because of this, you will occasionally see slight variations in tiles depending on the data source—a quintile might not contain exactly 20% of the population, but it will be very close.

With 5 or more tiles, it is a good idea to look at both quintiles I and II, rather than to focus only on quintile I.

Quintiles show relative usage, an important fact to remember. High indexes in the low usage quintiles mean that the target is less likely to use that medium, not that they are non-users of the medium. Even if a target is a relatively light user of magazines or television as a category, there will be specific magazines or TV programs that reach them well. Generally, media usage quintiles help planners in determining media mix, rather than the sole arbiter of whether to use a medium. An upscale professional/managerial type target for example, might be a very light user of television in general, but could be reached well using specific sports or financial programs.

EXHIBIT II

Frequent Flyer Program Members
Pop(000): 36378

	Mags	Nwsp	Radio	TV	Intrnt	Outdr
Quintile I(Heavy)						
(000)	8904	10790	6260	4151	12826	9193
Vert%	24.48	29.66	17.21	11.41	35.26	25.27
Horz%	21.01	25.46	14.78	9.80	30.31	21.69
Index	122	148	86	57	176	126
Quintile II						
(000)	8739	7854	7488	6053	10352	8839
Vert%	24.02	21.59	20.58	16.64	28.46	24.30
Horz%	20.63	18.54	17.67	14.28	24.43	20.87
Index	120	108	103	83	142	122
Quintile III						
(000)	7688	6932	8609	8424	7041	7628
Vert%	21.13	19.06	23.67	23.16	19.36	20.97
Horz%	18.14	16.35	20.32	19.88	16.61	18.00
Index	106	95	118	116	97	105
Quintile IV						
(000)	6718	6112	8017	8651	3339	6452
Vert%	18.47	16.80	22.04	23.78	9.18	17.74
Horz%	15.86	14.44	18.92	20.42	7.88	15.23
Index	92	84	110	119	46	89
Quintile V (Light)						
(000)	4329	4688	6004	9098	2819	4265
Vert%	11.90	12.89	16.50	25.01	7.75	11.72
Horz%	10.22	11.06	14.17	21.48	6.65	10.07
Index	60	64	83	125	39	59

Problems (See Exhibit II for all problems.)

1. How many Frequent Flyer Program Members are reported in *Newspaper Quintile V?*

2. Out of all Freq Flyers reported in the *Newspaper* column, what proportion (percentage) is made up of *Newspaper Quintile V* readers? Based on your experience with index numbers in previous exercises, you can calculate this percentage yourself. It's the ratio between the number of Freq Flyers reported at the intersection of Quintile V and Newspapers, and the sum of all the quintiles for the newspaper column. Show the math to prove you have chosen the the correct percentage from the crosstab.

3. You're media director working on the Motorola mobile phone business, and you need to evaluate magazines for your target audience, Frequent Flyer Program Members. After evaluating Exhibit II, what conclusion would you draw about magazine readership? Report index numbers to support your answer, and report the percentage of Freq Flyers in the *heaviest* magazine user quintile.

4. How is the index for Freq Flyers in the *heaviest* Magazine user Quintile calculated? Show your math. Tip: What percentage of adults are in the heaviest magazine user quintile? Review Exhibit I – see Gum Users graphic – and the *Application* section of this exercise.

5. Focusing exclusively on Quintile I, highlight the index numbers across all five media for your Freq Flyer target. Based on index numbers, rank all five media from high to low, and list the Quintile I index number for each medium.

6. Relatively speaking, which medium is used the *least* by Freq Flyers based on the indexes in the *bottom two quintiles*? (Report the numbers.) Tip: Review the text under the heading, "Twisted?"

7. Based on your answer to question 6, can Frequent Flyer Program Members still be reached by using this medium? There are two significant sections in the text that are relevant to light user Quintiles – cite both and provide complete answers.

COMPETITIVE SPENDING ANALYSIS AND SOV

Learning Objective

One of the first steps in developing a good media plan is to analyze the way your clients and their competitors allocate dollars to various media. Two major sources of competitive expenditures are TNS *Competitive Media Reporting* (CMR) and Nielsen's *Monitor Plus*. Most agencies have one of these sources for competitive reporting.

Once the competitive set for a brand has been determined, dollar expenditures in the various media classes can be used to evaluate both your own and your competitors' media mix, share of voice (SOV), and changes in annual expenditure. This helps provide a better understanding of your client's media environment.

Calculating Media Mix for Your Brand

The way media dollars are allocated is called the media mix. It is determined by calculating the proportion of ad dollars spent on your brand in each media category. As marketing director, assume you allocated your brand's annual advertising dollars in these four media:

Expenditures in $(000)				
Total	**Magazines**	**Network TV**	**Spot TV**	**Cable**
13,000	3,000	7,000	2,000	1,000

Media mix is calculated by dividing expenditure in a given media category by total expenditure. For example, here's how you would calculate the magazine part of the mix:

$$\text{Media Mix} = \frac{\text{brand medium expenditure}}{\text{brand total expenditure}} \times 100 = \frac{3000}{13000} \times 100 = 23\% \ (23.08 \text{ rounded})$$

Using this formula, the complete media mix showing the proportion of advertising dollars spent in each media class is calculated as shown below:

Total	**Magazines**	**Network TV**	**Spot TV**	**Cable**
100%	23%	54%	15%	8%

Calculating Share of Voice

Share of voice (SOV) is a common tool for competitive analysis. It shows a brand's strengths and weaknesses using individual media as well as overall position in the media marketplace. SOV is defined as a brand's percentage of total advertising dollars spent within a category. Share of voice can be applied to total expenditures or to a particular medium. The formula for share of voice is similar to the media mix formula, but the denominator of the equation is the spending total for the entire media category rather than total spending for the brand:

$$\text{Share of Voice} = \frac{\text{brand medium expenditure}}{\text{category medium expenditure}} \times 100$$

Exercise 10

Example: Your client, *MetroWerks* markets a specialized piece of software for developing video games. You have two competitors, *Borland*, and *Intel*. You have been provided with the following advertising expenditures, and have been asked to calculate each brand's share of voice for each media category. The equation in the box at right shows how the expenditures in Table I were used to calculate the Spot TV SOVs in Table II.

Table I

ADVERTISING EXPENDITURES $(000)					
Brand	**Total**	**Magazines**	**Net TV**	**Spot TV**	**Cable**
Borland	13,000	3,000	7,000	2,000	1,000
MetroWerks	17,000	5,000	9,000	**1,000**	2,000
Intel	18,000	1,000	14,000	3,000	0
Total Category	48,000	9,000	30,000	**6,000**	3,000

Table II

SHARE OF VOICE					
Brand	**Total**	**Magazines**	**Net TV**	**Spot TV**	**Cable**
Borland	27	33	23	33	33
MetroWerks	35	56	30	**17**	67
Intel	38	11	47	50	0
Total Category	100	100	100	100	100

MetroWerks Spot TV SOV:

$$\frac{1000}{6000} \times 100 = 17 \ (16.67 \ \text{rounded})$$

MetroWerks is responsible for about 17 percent of the activity in spot television, and about a third of overall category spending with a 35% Share of Voice. One cannot overestimate the value of data like this – SOV gives a brutally honest picture of your brand's advertising environment.

Exhibit I: Competitive Spending Problems

Exhibit I applies to the questions below. If you prefer working in Excel, this table is available as a spreadsheet on **mediaflightplan.com**. Click on **MFP Ground School**, and then look for Exercise 9.

EXHIBIT I

COPIER CATEGORY EXPENDITURES $(000)							
	Magazines	**Natl Nwsp**	**Outdoor**	**Net TV**	**Spot TV**	**Cable TV**	**Net Radio**
Canon Inc	7095.0	1011.2	212.1	4914.2	51.2	763.9	0.0
Compaq	374.1	545.9	0.0	0.0	0.0	0.0	0.0
Harris Corp	1116.2	124.0	0.0	0.0	11.6	357.0	0.0
Konica Corp	2558.8	129.8	11.1	0.0	30.3	878.2	0.0
Matsushita	172.1	0.0	0.0	0.0	4.6	0.0	0.0
Minolta	3902.2	0.0	3.3	0.0	43.2	0.0	0.0
Mita Co	1829.2	716.3	506.6	3222.7	134.0	405.1	778.8
Pitney Bowes	0.0	0.0	0.0	1128.9	0.8	411.1	595.1
Ricoh Co	1164.2	1471.9	0.0	1265.7	226.4	1345.9	0.0
Sharp Corp	2862.5	311.0	37.0	3525.7	1189.8	859.0	0.0
Toshiba Corp	0.0	0.0	0.0	0.0	24.6	0.0	0.0
Xerox Corp	37.2	635.6	2.4	547.2	0.7	0.0	0.0

Problems

1. Five copiers, Canon, Mita, Ricoh, Sharp, and Xerox, are targeted to the same market. Using Exhibit I, fill in media expenditure data and complete this "Big Five" table for the five brands listed.

"Big Five" Table: Media Expenditures

	Magazines	Natl Nwsp	Outdoor	Net TV	Spot TV	Cable TV	Net Radio	Total
Canon								
Mita								
Ricoh								
Sharp								
Xerox								
TOTAL								

2. Which of the five copier brands is the biggest media spender - i.e., which had the highest total advertising expenditures across all media? Name the brand and give the total amount below.

3. Which brand spent the most ad dollars in cable TV? Name the brand and the total amount.

4. Which brand spent the most ad dollars in Network TV? Name the brand and the total amount.

5. Using the figures you copied into the "Big Five" Table, calculate **Media Mix** (as percentages) for each copier brand. Enter proportions into the table below, rounded to one decimal place.

Media Mix								
	Magazines	Natl Nwsp	Outdoor	Net TV	Spot TV	Cable TV	Net Radio	Total
Canon								100.0
Mita								100.0
Ricoh								100.0
Sharp								100.0
Xerox								100.0

6. Using the figures in the "Big Five" Table, calculate *Share of Voice* for each copier brand. Enter SOV data into the table below. Round percentages to the nearest tenth.

	Magazines	Natl Nwsp	Outdoor	Net TV	Spot TV	Cable TV	Net Radio	Total
Share of Voice (SOV)								
Canon								
Mita								
Ricoh								
Sharp								
Xerox								
Total	100.0	100.0	100.0	100.0	100.0	100.0	100.0	100.0

7. The *Media Mix* table reveals percent of total budget that each brand allocates to each medium. In contrast, the *Share of Voice* table reveals which brand's "voice" dominates each medium, and which brand has less voice in each medium. Be sure to consult the correct table for questions below.

a) Xerox invested over 95 percent of total budget into two media. Relative to Xerox's media mix, name the two media and their respective percent of total budget.

b) What's significant about Xerox's SOV in these 2 media? Prove this with hard data.

c) Based on this SOV scenario, what is Xerox's best move? As media director, other than raising the budget, what advice would you give Xerox to help fix their problem?

8. Which brand has the highest share of voice in network TV? Lowest share in network TV? Give the specific shares for each:

9. Which brand has the highest share of voice in magazines? The lowest in magazines? Give specific shares for each:

10. Assume you are marketing director representing a totally new brand in the copy machine category, with a $6 million budget.

    a) Do you see any opportunities here to use unexploited media? Why or why not use them?

    b) Plan your own media strategy. Where would you spend the most, and why?

FACTOR "SPREADSHEETING" WITH A CALCULATOR

The easiest way to grasp the concept of ranking markets is to create your first factor "spreadsheet" using a hand-held calculator. After mastering this skill, you'll build on it using a spreadsheet, such as *Excel* with market weighting.

Learning Objective

This exercise demonstrates how spreadsheets can help evaluate and rank a group of markets, ranging from a handful to a hundred. Besides evaluating markets, factor spreadsheets are equally useful for evaluating media choices, media vehicles, etc. This is the first of three spreadsheet exercises; the next two focus on market weighting strategy.

Sharpen Your Media Math

The goal in this exercise is to sharpen your math skills, and help you think through the process as you design a simple market-ranking spreadsheet. Research published in academic journals indicates that professors and media planning professionals are concerned about weak math skills among entry-level planners. In one published study, Professor Sandra Utt, University of Memphis, said, "I was disappointed that a few of my students didn't even know how to get a percentage – I had to tell them to divide the big number into the little number." Dale Coons, Campbell-Ewald, lamented: "When interviewing interns, I'm often disappointed how some seem to tense up when I ask a few basic math questions. Students need to know that most marketing careers require a modest level of math and spreadsheet skill."

You can learn to use a spreadsheet and build confidence in your own math skills by designing a spreadsheet for every case study you write. Keep these case studies in your portfolio – they make good "show and tell" when the interviwer asks, "Do you have any experience?", or "Tell me about a major project in school."

How Factor Spreadsheets Work

Rhodes Bake 'n Serve Products markets a regional brand distributed in super stores. As marketing manager, you need to rank four cities based on their food sales potential in super stores. Data are available for four factors:

1. Total Population
2. Total Food Sales
3. Discretionary HH Income
4. Total Number of Super Stores

A factor spreadsheet reduces many pieces of data into a single "score" which can easily be compared across the markets.

Step 1: The first step is to build the factor spreadsheet, and calculate the ESTIMATED VALUE% of each city.

Calculating Estimated Value (EV%): The EV% is a ratio between the Total Across and the Total for that column. Look at the EV% for Reno in Exhibit I (8.8%). It is calculated like this:

$$215{,}201 \div 2{,}441{,}663 = 0.88 \times 100 = 8.8\%$$

Factor spreadsheets must be customized to fit each marketing problem. If you were marketing cosmetics instead of baked goods in super stores, which of the columns in Exhibit I would you replace? With what? An obvious replacement for cosmetics would be to replace "Total Food Sales" with "Total Cosmetic Sales". You might also want to replace "Total Pop" with "Female Teens".

Exercise 11

Exhibit I

	Total Pop (000)	Total Food $ Sales (000)	Discretionary $ HH Income (000)	Number of Stores	Total Across	Est. Value %
			Raw Number Factor Spreadsheet: Rhodes Bake 'n Serve Products			
Reno	190.0	170,000	45,000	11	215,201	8.8
Salt Lake	230.0	564,000	46,000	17	610,247	25.0
Portland	540.0	697,000	48,000	20	745,560	30.5
Seattle	596.0	821,000	49,000	29	870,625	35.7
Totals	1,556.0	2,252,000	188,000	77	2,441,633	100.0

Note: Est. Value % has been rounded for ease of discussion

This is a very small spreadsheet. Most spreadsheets contain multiple marketing factors across the top (columns) and run 50 to 100 markets (rows) deep.

Problem: Raw numbers in factor spreadsheets lead to unintentional weighting due to differences in scale. For example, in Reno, 11 stores will have very little impact because store count is overwhelmed by population. Population is reported in (000), but even so, the 190 figure is a factor of ten larger than the number of stores (hundreds vs tens). So the figures for population have an unintentional "weight" of 10 (10x10=100) compared to stores.

Solution: "Democratize" all raw numbers by converting them to percents. Note how data shown above for Pop, Food, HH Income and Number of Stores differ widely as numbers. Since the Number of Stores column has comparatively small numbers with only 2 digits, **Est. Value%** – the end result – would not change at all if you eliminated this entire column from the sheet.

Step 2: To create a more useful analysis, convert the raw number spreadsheet to percentages. For example, the Total Pop% for Reno is calculated using the numbers for Reno and the Total from Exhibit I:

190 ÷ 1,556 x 100 = 12% (rounded)

Exhibit II

	% Total Pop (000)	% Total Food $ Sales (000)	% Discretionary $ HH Income (000)	% Number of Stores	% Total Across	Est. Value %
			Percentage Factor Spreadsheet: Rhodes Bake 'n Serve Products			
Reno	12	8	24	14	58	14
Salt Lake	15	25	24	22	86	22
Portland	35	31	26	26	117	29
Seattle	38	36	26	38	138	35
Total	100	100	100	100	400	100

Note: All percents have been rounded to the nearest whole number for ease of discussion

The Estimated Values here (compared with the Raw Number Factor Spreadsheet) have changed significantly for all four markets, and especially for Reno. Reno increased 4 percentage points compared with the raw number spreadsheet. By using percentages in the Raw Number Factor Spreadsheet, all of the "boxcar" numbers have been put on the same scale, giving all the factors equal weight. For example, Seattle's **Food Sales** originally has six digits (821,000), and the Number of Stores column is expressed with only two digits: 29. When adding across, Seattle's Pop, Food Sales, and HH Income literally drown out the number of Grocery/Super stores. Once converted to percentages, both Food Sales and Number of Stores have the same scale and are placed on equal footing. Converting to percentages gives all the factors the same relative weight by washing out differences in scale.

Estimating Ad Budgets: Although the markets still happen to be ranked in the same order, the new Est. Value% changed each market's relative worth. In addition to ranking markets, EV% can also be used to help allocate budgets. With a total budget of $200,000, a planner could allocate the funds for Rhodes using the Est. Value% from Exhibit II by converting the percentages to decimals this way:

Reno estimated ad budget:	$200,000 X .14 = $28,000
Salt Lake estimated ad budget:	$200,000 X .22 = $44,000
Portland estimated ad budget:	$200,000 X .29 = $58,000
Seattle estimated ad budget:	$200,000 X .35 = $70,000

Chili's Niche Marketing Mini-Case

Niche marketing is an excellent strategy for building brand share in the Eating & Drinking/Restaurant category. Research conducted by Chili's discovered the Hispanic market niche (respondents of Mexican heritage = 42%) has the potential to increase national sales by 5% within two years. Research also suggests that the strongest appeal for this ethnic target audience would be one of Chili's most successful menu items – "Baby Back Ribs." Multi-ethnic, non-traditional promotions, combined with radio advertising, have been prepared to test Hispanic responses to Chili's ribs. Chili's will test in seven southwestern and southeastern markets.

To prepare for the test, your job is to analyze the syndicated data in Exhibit III. Using a calculator, create a simple factor spreadsheet to rank seven designated test markets: San Antonio, Jacksonville, Tucson, Albuquerque, Corpus Christi, St. Petersburg, and Orlando.

Follow the math models explained above (Exhibits I and II) to create your own factor spreadsheets for Chili's test market. Using the blank tables provided below, do the following:

1. Create a Raw Number Factor Spreadsheet for all 7 METRO AREAS. Use the blank table on the next page.

2. Fill in the factor spreadsheet using data provided in Exhibit III (last page of exercise). Follow these important instructions as you consult the three tables:

Population Table: Use **Total (000)** from the **Population** table. Remember numbers represent population in thousands (000). It is not necessary to convert the numbers before using them in a factor spreadsheet (and we won't), however, *it is absolutely necessary that you are consistent in recording data for a factor*. Don't use 1244.7 to record San Antonio and 291,300 for Corpus Christi. Use the same format for both. For this exercise, record the figures in thousands (e.g. 1,244.7 and 291.3, etc.) as reported in Exhibit III on the very last page of this exercise (next to *Weighting Factor Spreadsheets* exercise).

• **Retail Sales & Store Count**: There are eight columns of data in the **Retail Sales & Store Count** table. Look at all eight columns carefully. Choose *only one* of the eight columns in addition to the # of Chili's stores that best represents Chili's business.

• **Discretionary HH Income**: Use Discretionary HH Income. Again, record the numbers as reported in (000). For example, Discretionary HH Income San Antonio: 28,601

• Now, fill in the Total Across and calculate the Estimated Value % as shown above. Round EV%s to one decimal place

Exercise 11

Raw Number Factor Spreadsheet

Markets	Pop (000)	Choice from Retail Sales:	Store Count	Discretionary HH Income (000)	Total Across	Estimated Value %
San Antonio						
Jacksonville						
Tucson						
Albuquerque						
Corpus Christi						
St Petersburg						
Orlando						
Total						

3. Create a **Percent Conversion Spreadsheet**. Convert all raw data from step 1 to the spreadsheet below. Round to one decimal place – for example: 24.9% or 3.6%.

Percent Conversion Factor Spreadsheet

Markets	% Pop (000)	%Choice from Retail Sales:	% Store Count	% Discretionary HH Income (000)	% Total Across	Estimated Value %
San Antonio						
Jacksonville						
Tucson						
Albuquerque						
Corpus Christi						
St Petersburg						
Orlando						
Total						

4. Based on the **Estimated Value %** column, rank order all seven markets from strongest to weakest. This list of markets will be based on your answers to question 3 above.

5. a) After the percent conversion, only San Antonio stays in the same position-second. All the remaining markets changed their ranking in the percent conversion. List them showing the old EV% ranking (based on raw numbers) and their new EV% ranking after percent conversions.

Market	Old EV% Rank	New EV% Rank

b) Why did this happen? (Tip: Review the text below Exhibit II.)

6. Total advertising budget for the seven metro markets is $1,500,000. Based on the Estimated Values (**EV%**) from the Percent Conversion Factor Spreadsheet, calculate the total advertising budget allocated to each of the seven markets, and rank them from 1 to 7. For example, if one market had 11.7% EV, then multiply .117 X $1,500,000 in order to find that market's budget ($175,500).

Exercise 11

Exhibit III

Population

| Metro Market | Total (000) | % U.S | Median Age Of Pop. | % of Pop. by Age Group | | | | HHs (000) |
				18-24 Years	25-34 Years	35-49 Years	50 & Over	
San Antonio	1,244.7	0.410	40.1	8.3	14.2	17.8	38.9	53.9
Jacksonville	798.1	0.270	38.3	8.1	14.0	18.2	36.1	70.5
Tucson	521.7	0.170	33.0	11.6	17.3	20.0	26.1	365.9
Albuquerque	488.6	0.160	32.1	11.4	17.1	21.0	24.0	49.3
Corpus Christi	291.3	0.097	31.2	12.3	17.5	20.7	22.7	128.6
St. Petersburg	274.5	0.091	51.1	6.7	11.7	15.1	51.1	115.7
Orlando	215.0	0.072	40.5	8.7	14.4	17.3	39.6	838.9

Retail Sales $(ooo) and Stores

Metro Market	Elec & Cons Prods	Grocery & Super store	Eating/ Drinking & Restrnt	General Mdse.	Furniture & Appliance	Auto Parts & Access	Phar macy	# Chili's Stores
San Antonio	1,170.0	257.0	152.3	899.0	117.7	250.7	40.0	17
Jacksonville	123.8	261.5	109.4	150.8	71.3	249.8	49.3	12
Tucson	7,210.4	1,385.9	1,046.9	838.7	321.6	1,996.0	190.1	12
Albuquerque	848.3	129.3	143.7	113.7	44.7	231.3	28.6	14
Corpus Christi	2,009.4	408.6	249.4	332.5	109.3	497.3	57.1	9
St. Petersburg	2,200.9	418.7	285.0	245.5	204.2	517.1	95.5	12
Orlando	13,442.9	2,903.6	1,742.0	1,760.5	874.1	3,132.8	461.2	10

Income

| Metro Market | Total HHI (000) | Discretionary HH Income $ (000) | % of Households By Income Group (A) $10,000-$19,999 (B) $20,000-$34,999 (C) $35,000-$49,999 (D) $50,000 & Over | | | | Household Buying Power Index |
			A	B	C	D	
San Antonio	28,702.3	28,601	25.8	26.4	12.0	15.4	0.0602
Jacksonville	27,238.6	28,300	31.4	25.9	9.4	7.9	0.0652
Tucson	28,542.2	26,188	23.4	27.0	16.7	17.1	0.4085
Albuquerque	26,686.1	22,702	29.8	25.8	11.6	7.6	0.0456
Corpus Christi	23,889.2	23,420	22.8	26.3	16.6	15.0	0.1301
St. Petersburg	31,164.5	33,818	23.3	23.6	14.4	15.9	0.0847
Orlando	25,703.9	24,469	26.5	26.8	14.6	14.4	0.8236

WEIGHTING FACTOR SPREADSHEETS

This tutorial requires a spreadsheet (like Microsoft Excel 2011). Those who are familiar with Excel will find they know other methods to copy and format. This tutorial is written so that someone less familiar with Excel can complete the exercise successfully.

Now that you've learned the basics of factor spreadsheets using a calculator, this exercise introduces two new concepts: (1) How to design a marketing factor spreadsheet using a program like Excel. (2) How to apply "weight," and how it can be used as a tool to manipulate the outcome of a marketing factor spreadsheet.

Since you are familiar with the data from the previous exercise, you'll use the same data here. The first part of the exercise will be familiar; you'll create a raw number spreadsheet, then convert it to percentages. *The EV%s you obtain using a program like Excel may vary slightly from the results you obtained on your calculator.*

Learning Objective

Learn the concept of "weighting" and ranking markets. Based on evaluation of marketing/media columns in a factor spreadsheet, marketers may want to give added value to exceptional columns of data. The objective in this exercise is to learn how to give extra weight to a column of data that is considered more important than the rest of the columns.

Understanding Weighting

Its a good bet that some marketing factors in your spreadsheet are more important than others. If one or two of the variables are judged to be exceptional in value, they can be "loaded" with extra weight. Weighting of variables will affect the Estimated Value percents once the spreadsheet is calculated, giving those variables the emphasis their importance demands. Emphasis can be controlled in two ways—by weighting only those variables considered to have exceptional value, and by varying the amount of weight applied to a variable. It might be tempting to weight every factor, but avoid this line of thinking. Weighting everything is like weighting nothing. If a spreadsheet has five or six variables, typically one or two variables should be singled out for extra weight.

Frequently Asked Questions about Weighting

Some questions frequently come up as factor spreadsheets are put together. The guidance that follows will help you as you think about the strategies and objectives you are trying to accomplish as you build your factor spreadsheet.

Why is it necessary to weight in the first place? It is not always necessary, but weighting is often helpful in ranking markets. A seasoned marketer once remarked, "I have never met a marketing spreadsheet that could not be improved by weighting." What he means is that we can usually assume that all columns in a spreadsheet do not have equal value in helping us rank markets. Once we understand that a spreadsheet is a *strategic tool,* we can use it to manipulate the output (the EV%s or Estimated Value % Column) to help us make some kind of marketing decision.

Weighting can be useful by putting extra emphasis on the most important column (or columns) of data in a spreadsheet. Of course, the "most important column" is a judgment call.

How do I know which column to weight? In most all spreadsheets, at least one of the columns is more valuable than the others. To discover that column, consider "trashing" all the columns in the spreadsheet except one. In other words, if you were forced to live with only one column of data to rank your markets, *which column can you NOT live without?* Decide which column is indispensable, and you'll know which column to weight.

Why use exponential weighting? There are many ways to weight data and calculate estimated value. Some of these have mathematical drawbacks and are best avoided. Using exponentiation (raising numbers to a power) and summing across factors avoids several issues.

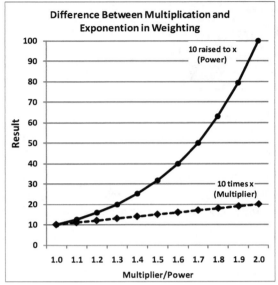

While this isn't a math exercise, a couple of quick points will illustrate some of the reasons we prefer exponents for weighting and summing for EVs.

Thinking about weighting for a moment, and you will realize if a single factor is simply doubled or tripled, the new value will still get lost when it is summed with several other factors—and testing has shown that there is little movement when using simple multiplication. The chart to the right shows how exponentiation overcomes this problem. In a sense, the two lines could represent two different factors, each with the same value, 10. You can see the difference in separation as one is weighted with multiplication (lower, dotted line) and one is weighted with exponentiaion (upper, solid line) with the same weights. The factor that is exponentially weighted by squaring (raising to a power of 2) is significantly higher than the one that was simply doubled. Exponentiation allows weighting that survives the summing of many factors to compute EV values.

The factor spreadsheets we'll build use summing to combine the factors for EV calculation. Some advocate multiplication, but this has a serious flaw. Can you think of what it might be? What would happen to a market that had five high value factors and a single factor that was zero if they were multiplied together? The result would be zero, implying the market had no value at all.

Building a Factor Spreadsheet using a Spreadsheet Program

These instructions were designed for Microsoft Excel 2010. Commands for Excel 2003 in particular may be in a different location than indicated here. You can use another spreadsheet you prefer, but you will have to find the equivalent commands yourself. As you work this factor spreadsheet, be aware that errors can easily creep in through typos or misplacement of formulas. To help monitor your progress, you may want to double-check each input and mark each step as you complete it, and save your work frequently.

This tutorial makes use of several Excel features. The image below shows where the "Menu" and "Ribbon" areas of Excel are. Your screen may be somewhat different depending on how it was set up. Though some commands are available in other places, everything we will use is available in the ribbon when the Home menu tab is selected as shown. Commands are organized into "Groups" on the ribbon, like "Alignment".

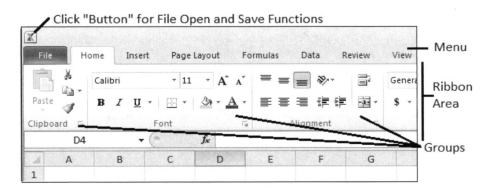

Before you start, make a weighting decision: Which column should be weighted in the Chili's spreadsheet? Look over the four columns of data you used in the previous exercise and decide which one you think is the most important.

Write your answer here:_____

Part I: Begin with Raw Number Spreadsheet

• **Step 1**: Open a new spreadsheet. In cell A1, type "**Chili's Raw Number Data**" to title this area of the spreadsheet. Click A1 again, and on the Home menu tab, click the **B** (bold) button to bold the heading. Be sure you title each new area of your factor spreadsheet as this will help clarify what you are doing.

• **Step 2**: In spreadsheet programs, rows are horizontal – columns are vertical. Individual cells are found at the intersection of the row and column indicated. For example, A3 is at the intersection of column A and row 3. Starting at column A on the far left, in row 3, type the following headings in the cells indicated. The complete heading won't show, but we'll fix that in a moment.

Cell	Column Heading
A3	Markets
B3	Population
C3	Eat&Drink Rest Sales
D3	# of Chili's Stores
E3	Discretionary HH Income
F3	Total Across
G3	EV%

To make the entire text of the headings show, first highlight the cells A3 to G3 by clicking in the middle of A3 and dragging across to G3. Now find the "Wrap Text" command in the Alignment group on the ribbon and click it. Your headings will now take several lines, but all the text should be showing. Also click the **B** (bold) command to bold the headings.

Now, widen the columns where necessary to make the text fit better. At the top of each column is a title letter (A,B,C, etc) with boundary lines on either side. Move the cursor over the boundary line until it turns into a vertical bar with a double headed arrow. Click the boundary to grab it, and move it until you are satisfied, then release the mouse button. You will probably want to widen the *Population* column until the heading fits on a single line, and the other headings until they fit comfortably on two lines.

The weighting variable chosen for this example is "# of Chili's Stores". Eating/Drinking & Restaurant Sales (this would be the category sales data for Chili's) could also be justified. To keep us all on the same page, follow the directions here and weight *# of Chili's Stores* even if you chose another factor. Chili's has research on store vs. brand sales in each market, and knows that number of stores is related to Chili's brand sales.

• **Step 3**: Using Exhibit III from the previous exercise, enter all seven markets under the *Markets* heading, beginning with cell **A4**.

- San Antonio should be in cell A4, Jacksonville in cell A5, etc. Cell A10 should be Orlando.

- Type *Total* in cell **A11**

- If necessary, widen column A by grabbing its boundary and moving it so that the market names fit comfortably in the column.

• **Step 4**: Using Exhibit III from the previous exercise, enter the data into the appropriate cells. For example, in cell **B5**, type *1,244.7* for San Antonio's population. Reminder: the heading of the table indicates that the units are (000), so that the 1244.7 represents 1,244,700. As you create your own factor spreadsheets, you can use whatever format you wish, as long as you are consistent within a factor. As long as you are consistent, the results of the factor spreadsheet will be the same. For purposes of this exercise, type in the numbers from Exhibit III as you see them. You may have to widen some of the columns, see the box below.

• Type in the data for all columns. Here's an easy guide; double-check entries for accuracy:

For this factor...	Use this column of data from Exhibit III
Population	Total Population
Eat/Drink & Rest Sales	Eating/Drinking & Restrnt
# of Chili's Stores	# of Chili's Stores
Disc HH Income	Discretionary HH Income

What to do when you get something like 1.2E+11 or ####
At times you may enter values or get calculated results that are too big to display in the cell. When this happens, Excel will first try to represent the number in scientific notation (something like 1.23E+11). If that won't fit, you'll get #####. In either case, you can get the numbers to display by making the column wider.

Part II: Using Excel's Summation Tool

The **Σ Auto Sum** button is found on the Home tab ribbon at the far right in the Editing group (It is also on the Formulas tab). The Σ button will automatically sum a row or column.

• **Step 5**: Click on cell **F4**. Now click on the **Σ button**, and then press [Enter]. Cell F4 should now read 30,015.0. (Widen the column if necessary.)

To show commas in all the numbers, highlight the entire block of data from **B4 to F11** (not all of those cells currently contain data). On the Home menu tab, click the **Format** button in the Cells group, and select *Format Cells* from the dropdown menu (very last item). Click the *Number* tab, check the *Use 1000 seperator (,) box*, and enter *1* in the *Decimal Places* box. Then click OK.

• **Step 6**: **Shortcut for summing remaining rows**: Click on cell **F4**. In the dark outline around F4 in the lower right corner is a tiny square box. We'll call it **CB** – short for "copy box". Position the mouse over the CB – once you have the mouse positioned over the bottom right hand corner of the cell, the cursor changes from a hollow cross into a solid "plus sign". Click on the CB, (don't release the mouse,) and drag down to cell **F10**. Release the mouse. Rows 5 through 10 should now be totaled. You may need to widen the column a bit.

• **Step 7**: **To sum columns**: Click on cell **B11**, click Σ and hit [Enter]. Cell B11 should now read 3,833.9.

Shortcut: Clicking the Auto Sum button automatically puts the formula =SUM(B4:B10) into A11. Since we need to do the exact same sum in the other cells in the Total row, we can copy A11 to the other columns, and Excel will adjust the formula to sum the correct data for us automatically. Highlight cell **B11**, click on CB and drag across to cell **F11**. Release the mouse button. Now, TOTAL figures appear for all columns.

Part III: Calculating Estimated Value % (EV %)

EV% is a ratio between the row's *Total Across* number and the sum of all the rows' *Total Across* number (in F11). EV%s represent the relative value of each market.

• **Step 8**: To get the EV%, divide cell F4 by cell F11 and multiply by 100. Put cursor in cell **G4** and type the following:

   • **=F4/$F$11*100** then press [Enter]. You just divided cell F5 by cell F11, and multiplied by 100 to convert to a percentage. The $ signs are important. They make the demonimator of the formula "absolute" so that it always refers to F12 when it is copied. If you leave them out, you will get errors when you copy the formula down.

- Click on cell **G4**

- Click on **CB** (Tiny bottom "copy box")

- Drag down to cell **G11**

- Now format your percentages with one decimal place. Begin by highlighting all the cells in column G, from **G4** to **G11**. Click *Format*, and in the dropdown box, select Format Cells. Click the Number tab, then select the category *Number*. Choose 1 decimal place in the box to the right. The sample box should show your result with one decimal place (e.g. 15.4)

- Now all of the EV% data should expressed as a percentage with one decimal place. Cell **G11** should read 100.0

- **Save your work!**

Part IV: Converting Raw Numbers (Columns B, C, D and E) into Percentages

• **Step 9**: In cell **A16**, type "Chili's Percentage Data". Bold it using the B button in the Font group.

• **Step 10**: Go to first table "Chili's Raw Data," highlight all column headings (A3-G3)

• **Step 11**: With the headings highlighted, click *Copy* from the Clipboard group on the ribbon (first group on left)

• **Step 12:** Click on cell **A18.** Now find the *Paste* command in the Clipboard group on the ribbon, just to the left of the Copy command, and click it. Excel will copy the headings from the previous table, including formatting.
- Now highlight the markets and Total label in cells **A4 to A11**. Click *Copy* again.
- Click on cell **A19**, then click the *Paste* command.
- DO NOT copy or paste any of the numbered data.

• **Step 13**: To convert to percentages, start by dividing San Antonio's pop (1,244.7) by the Total (3,833.9) and multiplying by 100 to get a percentage.
- In cell **B19**, type this division formula: **=B4/$B$11*100** then hit Enter (remember the $ signs!)
- Click cell **B19**, then click and hold on **CB**, then drag to **B26**
- Cells B20 through B27 should still be highlighted. If not, highlight them
- Click *Format*, and select *Format Cells* as before
- Make sure you are in the Number tab
- Click *Number*
- Choose 1 decimal place and click OK
- Total Down for column B should now be 100.0

• **Step 14**: Columns C, D, and E must also be expressed as percents. Follow the procedure in Step 13, but remember to change the formula to match the column. For example, the formula in cell **C19** will be **=C5/$C$12*100**. Don't forget the $ signs!

Part V: Summing the Total Across Column

• **Step 15**:
- Highlight cell **F19**
- Hit the **Σ button** and hit [Enter]
- Select cell **F19**, click on CB, and drag down to total all rows

Exercise 12

Part VI: Calculating the ESTIMATED VALUE % (EV %)

- **Step 16**: Put cursor in cell **G19** and type: **=F19/$F$26*100** then hit Enter

- **Step 17**: Click on cell **F19**; click on CB and drag down to **F26** to get EV% for all rows

Part VII: Exponential weighting

You will be weighting the same data two times, but each time you will use a different weight.

- **Step 18**: In cell **A30**, enter "**Chili's Weighted Data**". Click A30 again and bold it with the bold button.

- **Step 19**: In cell **A31**, enter "**Column Weight:**" and bold it. In B31, C31, D31 and E31, enter the number 1. Highlight these four cells and format to one decimal place (Click on **Format** in Cells group, select *Format Cells* on drop down, then click on *Number* for Category and enter 1 for *Decimal Places*, then click OK.)

- **Step 20**: Now copy and paste all column and row headings . . .
  - Copy **A18** through **G18** (**Markets**, **Population**, etc.) and paste at cell **A32**.
  - Copy the markets – **San Antonio** through **Total** from cells **A19** to **A26** into **A33**.

- **Step 21**: This step will set up weighting. Go to cell **B33**.

  - Enter the formula **=B19^B$31** *There is only one $ in this formula!*

  > The ^ symbol (shift-6 on most keyboards) is the exponentiation operator in Excel.

  - Select **B33**, click the **CB**, and drag the formula *across* to **E33**. Let go of the mouse.
  - Grab the **CB** again (four cells should be outlined) and drag it *down* to **E39**.
  - All of the rows except *Total* should have a formula in the four data columns.

- **Step 22**: Insert the formulas for Total Across. Select **F33**, then click the **Σ button** and [Enter]. This time, click on **F33** and use the **CB** to drag the formula down to Orlando (**F39**), and stop. Do not copy down to the *Total* line. Now, highlight cell **F40** and click the **Σ button** again. This will give you a TOTAL in the Total Across column of 400. There won't be totals in any other column.

- **Step 23**: Calculate EV% again. Click on cell **G33**. Type the formula **=F33/$F$40*100** and [Enter].
  - Click on **G33** and format to one decimal place.
  - Now, click on **G33**, grab **CB**, and drag down to **G40**. The Total for the EV% column should be 100.0

- **Step 24**: Now you can play "what-if". Change the weight above # Chili's Stores (in cell **D31**) from 1.0 to 1.5 and watch what happens to the EV%'s. Did you notice the EV% for San Antonio changed from 17.8 to 20.4?

Part VIII: Saving Scenarios and Sorting

The *Chili's Weighted Data* table we just created is handy because we can try different weighting scenarios without creating a new table each time. It is only necessary to change the weights at the top of the columns.

However, it has a large drawback—Excel cannot properly sort it. If you try, the market labels will be sorted in the correct order according to EV%, but the EV%s do not move along with the labels. This is because there is no way to tell Excel to modify the formula structure during a sort.

We need a way to save different scenarios in a manner that allows us to sort them. We will need the original *Chili's Raw Number Data* (which we already have), and the *Chili's Weighted Data* table with *# of Chili's Stores* weighted at 1.5 and 2.0 for the next exercise.

The next steps will show you how to save and sort scenarios.

• Step 25: Saving Different Scenarios of the Chili's Weighted Data
There are many ways to do things in Excel. You may know some shortcuts which you can use later. For now, follow along so that you see exactly what is happening.

Each time we save a scenario, the first paste will copy the labels and their formatting, the second will copy numeric values and their formats.

- Change your weights to match these if they don't already— B31: 1.0; C31: 1.0; D31: 1.5; and E31: 1.0
- Highlight the entire table, including titles, headings and weights (**A45 to G55**).
- On the home menu ribbon, click *Copy*
- Click on cell A60. That is where we will save the 1.5 weight scenario.
- Click *Paste*. This copies the labels, but the formulas are all wrong.
- Immediately, click the little arrow underneath the Paste Clipboard icon
- Select *Paste Special* (near the bottom) from the dropdown.
- In the dialog box, select *Values and number formats* on the right hand side and click [OK].

Your scenario is saved, formatted, and is now sortable, since there are no more formulas. That (obviously) means you can't change it anymore. But you still have your original live copy of the table to make changes with.

• Step 26: Create the 2.0 weight scenario, and save it:
- Change the weight in **D31** to 2.0
- Highlight the entire table again, including titles, headings and weights (**A45 to G55**).
- On the home menu ribbon, click *Copy*
- Click on cell A73.
- Click *Paste*.
- Immediately, click the little arrow underneath the Paste Clipboard icon
- Select *Paste Special* (near the bottom) from the dropdown.
- In the dialog box, select *Values and number formats* on the right hand side and click [OK].

Now that you know how to save a scenario, you can create as many as you wish, saving them following this pattern.

• Step 27: Sorting Markets Into Rank Order
It would be nice to have our scenarios sorted in rank order, with the highest EV% markets at the top. *Only do this on a saved scenario, **never** on your live table!*

- Highlight the column headings and data, but not the Total row in your 1.5 weight scenario (**A47 to G54**).
- On the home menu ribbon, click the little down arrow under *Sort and Filter* (under funnel icon)
- Select *Custom Sort*, the third option.
- Make sure the *My data has headers* checkbox in the upper right is checked.
- In the *Column Sort by* dropdown, pick *EV%*. In the *Order* dropdown, pick *Largest to smallest*
- Click [OK]
- Your data should now be sorted in the proper order, with San Antonio first and Corpus Christi last.

• Step 28: Sort the 2.0 weighted scenario following the same directions, but highlighting cells **A62 to G69**

• Step 30: Print and Save

- Click the round "Windows Button" and select Print. This exercise will print on two sheets.
- Save your printouts for the next exercise.
- **Save your work!**

INTERPRETING WEIGHTING RESULTS

You will need the printouts of your factor spreadsheet results from the previous exercise to answer these questions.

Learning Objective

The purpose of weighting a spreadsheet is to manipulate the ranking of markets thereby changing the outcome of the spreadsheet. This exercise tests your understanding of exponential weighting theory.

1. What are the differences in the relative value between the three spreadsheets after exponential weighting was applied? Focus on the EVs for these two markets:

Market	Chili's Percentage Data EV%	1.5 Weight Scenario EV%	2.0 Weight Scenario EV%
San Antonio			
Orlando			

2. If advertising budgets were allocated based on the results of **# of Chili's Stores** weighted at 1.5 (*1.5 Weight Scenario*), which markets gain ad dollars compared to the unweighted EVs (*Chili's Percentage Data*), and by how much? (Your answer should be expressed in EV% points gained.)

3. If advertising budgets were allocated based on the results of **# of Chili's Stores** weighted at 1.5, which markets lose ad dollars compared to the unweighted EV%? (Look for markets whose EV% declined)

Exercise 13

Exhibit I
Original Unweighted Budget

Previously, you calculated ad budgets for all seven markets based on unweighted EV%s, shown below.

Market	EV%	EV% Decimal		$ Ad Budget		$ Budget Allocation
San Antonio	17.9	.179	X	1,500,000	=	$ 268,394
Jacksonville	13.2	.132	X	1,500,000	=	197,992
Tucson	17.4	.174	X	1,500,000	=	261,019
Albequerque	11.2	.112	X	1,500,000	=	168,694
Corpus Christi	9.3	.093	X	1,500,000	=	139,660
St Petersburg	11.7	11.7	X	1,500,000	=	175,474
Orlando	19.3	.193	X	1,500,000	=	288,768
Total						$1,500,000

4. Using the original $1.5 million total budget shown in Exhibit I, calculate a new ad budget for each of the 7 markets using EV% resulting from the 2.0 weight you applied.

Market	Weight 2.0 Scenario EV%	EV% Decimal	Total Ad Budget	Budget Allocation
San Antonio			1,500,000	$
Jacksonville			1,500,000	
Tucson			1,500,000	
Albuquerque			1,500,000	
Corpus Christi			1,500,000	
St. Petersburg			1,500,000	
Orlando			1,500,000	
				Total $1,500,000

5. Using the budget results from your calculations above, how much ad budget did San Antonio, Albuquerque, and St. Petersburg gain compared with the original unweighted ad budget in Exhibit I?

San Antonio: Albuquerque: St Petersburg:

6. Based on exponential weighting, some markets sacrifice a portion of their ad budget to benefit stronger markets. In this case, how much did the 3 gaining markets obtain at the expense of four other markets? Calculate the difference for all sacrificing markets compared to unweighted EV allocations in Exhibit I.

Sacrificing Market	$ Difference From Exhibit I
Jacksonville	
Tucson	
Corpus Christi	
Orlando	
Total Given to Gaining Mkts	

NATIONAL + SPOT HEAVY-UP MEDIA BUYS

Learning Objective

To grasp the dynamic relationship between national and spot media, and how they impact each other when combined. Used alone, spot market buying gives marketers the freedom to concentrate media weight in specific geographic regions. In contrast to national buys that cover the entire US, spot buys range from one market to dozens. However, a more dynamic media force can be created when the two are combined intelligently and strategically.

Examples for strategic uses of spot market media planning

Regional Brands: If your brand is marketed in only one or two cities, spot market planning lets you buy media market-by-market, and add markets as you grow. Many well-known brands started out very small, marketing in only a few cities, adding markets as they grew. Red Lobster is a classic example; founder Bill Darden originated the concept of casual seafood dining with a single store in Lakeland, Florida and by the early 70s had expanded into the southeast. As he expanded his store count from coast to coast, his spot advertising campaign grew one market at a time until he was into over 50 markets. That's when he went national, and now has over 400 stores.

Test Markets: It is much cheaper to "test the waters" in a few isolated markets to discover a new brand's potential for success. Spot buying allows you to limit your test market to one or two cities.

National With Spot Heavy-Up: Due to regional differences in culture, lifestyle, climate, etc., national brands are rarely consumed equally in all metro markets. For example, if you are assigned to create a national marketing plan for Snickers Frozen Ice Cream Bars, a common marketing practice is to add heavy-up weight in markets with above average category or brand potential. Houston, Texas, has a high CDI (186) and strong BDI (157) for frozen confections. (See Exhibit I) In addition to the national media weight (300 GRPs); the Snickers brand manager might give Houston a heavy-up dose of media weight—say, an extra 100 GRPs. Spot markets with high potential often get an advertising boost.

Exhibit 1

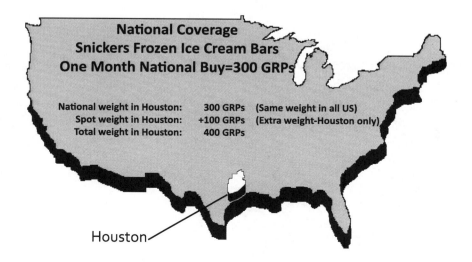

National Coverage
Snickers Frozen Ice Cream Bars
One Month National Buy=300 GRPs

National weight in Houston:	300 GRPs	(Same weight in all US)
Spot weight in Houston:	+100 GRPs	(Extra weight-Houston only)
Total weight in Houston:	400 GRPs	

Houston

You can think of a spot buy as a second media plan integrated into the national plan. Heavy-up markets are endowed with extra media weight in addition to the national weight that already covers them. The effect is that reach/frequency will be higher in the spot markets than in the rest of the US. *Media Flight Plan* will help you see this more clearly as you complete this exercise.

Problems

Your assignment is to create a national media plan integrated with a spot plan for PF Chang's China Bistro. PF Chang's sales are strong nationally, but 12 markets in the Northwest and Mountain West regions demonstrate excellent growth potential.

Step 1: Campaign Basics

Go to mediaflightplan.com, launch Media Flight Plan and enter the following data:

- *Target Demo:* For Gender, select **[Adults]**, then **Age Groups 18 through 49**. To exit, click **[OK]**.

- *Campaign Settings:* For Campaign Scope, click **[Both National and Spot]**. For your Starting Month, select **[June]**. This campaign will run for only three months (June, July, and August) as a test bed for PF Chang's market research team. To exit, click **[OK]**.

Bend, Or	Grand Junction, CO	Salt Lake City, UT
Colorado Springs, CO	Las Vegas, NV	Seattle-Tacoma, WA
Denver, CO	Medford, OR	Spokane, WA
Eugene, OR	Portland, OR	Yakima, WA

- *Spot Markets:* Click **[Spot Markets]** and select the 12 markets listed in the box below.

- *Budget:* Click on the **[Budget]** tab and type **8000000** into **Total Budget Amount**, and hit **[Enter.]** Make sure 8000000 (with 6 zeros) shows on the bottom line, **Total Media Budget**. Click **[OK]** to exit.

Step 2: National Goals

Click on **[Goals]** tab. Beginning in June, enter the Reach/Freq goals for all 3 months (see table below). Take note that *MFP* automatically calculates GRPs and Share for you. Write down the GRPs in the table below.

National Goals Table

Month	Reach	Freq	GRPs
June	70	4	_____
July	75	5	_____
August	80	5	_____

Step 3: Spot Goals

You should still be in Goals. Enter the Spot Goals shown below – be sure to begin with June. When done, take note of the numbers displayed in the **[AD] GRPs** column. Write all three **[AD] GRPs** into the table below. [AD] GRPs=ADDITIONAL GRPs needed to achieve the higher Reach/Frequency goals in your 12 spot markets.

Spot Goals Table

Month	Reach	Freq	[AD] GRPs
June	80	6	_____
July	85	7	_____
August	90	8	_____

Step 4: National & Spot Dynamic – A Key Concept

Complete the math below to learn how Media Flight Plan calculates [AD] GRPs. You can verify your answers here – NATL GRPs and [AD] GRPs should agree with the GRPs in both tables above.

Month	Spot Reach	X	Spot Freq	=	Spot GRPs	-	Natl GRPs	=	[AD] GRPs
June	80	X		=		-		=	
July	85	X		=		-		=	
August	90	X		=		-		=	

Step 5: Total GRP weight delivered to the Spot Markets is higher than shown in the [AD] GRPs column. When you "heavy-up" in spot markets, MFP combines the [AD] Spot GRP weights with pre-existing National GRP weights to produce the required weight. To prove this mathematically, you can calculate the total GRP weights actually delivered to the 12 spot markets each month. Look at Exhibit I to see how Total Weight is calculated using Houston as an example, and complete the following table with the GRPs from steps 2 and 3.

	Nat'l GRPs		Spot [AD] GRPs		Total GRP weight in 12 Spot Markets
June	_____	+	_____	=	_____
July	_____	+	_____	=	_____
August	_____	+	_____	=	_____

Step 6: GRP Experiment

Click on the **[Goals]** tab. On the Spot Goals side of the screen, find June and make these changes:

    Reach   = 70
    Frequency = 4

A) Did you notice what changed? Write the new [AD] GRPs for June below.

    New [AD] GRP for June: _____

B) What happened? If you compare both National and Spot goals, note that June has identical Reach/Frequency goals in both screens. Explain why spot goals must exceed national goals. Prove your answer using an example with numbers. (Tip: See Exhibit 1)

Step 7: Change your Spot Goals in June back to the original spot goals.

    Reach   = 80
    Frequency = 6

Save your work now. Data from this exercise will be used in the next exercise. (Click the SAVE button displayed in upper right corner of screen).

Step 8: How MFP Calculates BUDGET SHARE for each month

Monthly budget Share is a simple calculation done automatically by Media Flight Plan at the moment you enter your Reach/Frequency goals. Each month's budget share is a percentage displayed for both National and Spot buys.

Exercise 14

Focus on the National Goals Budget Share for the month of June. It is a ratio between two figures. Here's the formula:

$$\frac{\text{National GRPs for June}}{\text{Sum of all National Goals GRPs} + \text{all Spot Goals [AD]GRPs}} \times 100 = \text{June Share}$$

The share calculated by MFP is used to estimate the dollars available to meet your goal in June. You may actually need to spend more or less to accomplish your reach/frequency goal in any given month.

Step 9: Applying the formula to calculate budget Share for June:

National GRPs

Calculate the SUM of all **National Goals GRPs** below: June _____

July _____

Aug _____

Sum _____

Spot [AD] GRPs

Calculate the SUM of all **Spot Goals [AD] GRPs** below: June _____

July _____

Aug _____

Sum _____

Apply the formula shown above to calculate National budget Share for June.

Using the same logic, calculate Spot budget Share for June and show your math.

STRETCHING YOUR MEDIA BUDGET

Learning Objective

This exercise will help you discover creative ways to stretch your ad budget. You will have a stronger working knowledge about theoretical goal setting, and how to think creatively when faced with real-world marketing challenges.

Reach/Frequency goals provide a good starting point

As you may recall from the MFP tutorial, the reach/frequency goals you type into the goals screens are very rough estimates, and can always be adjusted up or down as needed. After reach/frequency goals are converted to GRPs, you can begin buying GRPs in the various media. Remember, however, that these estimated GRPs may or may not achieve your reach/frequency goal after the buy is made. Every buy is an experiment.

Problem Setup

This exercise builds on the *PF Chang's* mini-case you started previously. If you saved it, load the file and go directly to Step 1. (Click **[LOAD]** at top of MFP screen). If not, go back to the exercise *National+Spot Heavy Up Media Buys* and enter the following data into *MFP*:

1. All the Campaign Basics for *PF Chang's China Bistro*
2. Goals: Enter all National and Spot Reach/Frequency goals for *PF Chang's*

Step 1: National and Spot Shares

Click on the **[Goals]** tab. Write shares below for both National and Spot Goals:

	National Goals Share	Spot Goals Share
June	_____	_____
July	_____	_____
August	_____	_____

Step 2: Tweaking the Budget

- Click on **[Budget]**. On the bottom line, Total Media Budget should be $8 million.
- Change the Total Budget to $10.00. (Ten dollars is obviously absurd, but go along for now).

Step 3: Nothing Changes

Click on **Goals**. Compare the budget shares (both National and Spot) with the percents you reported above. Has anything changed? It should *not* have. Why do budget Shares remain constant even after your total budget drops to ten dollars? *MFP* is indifferent to whatever number you type into the Budget, from a penny to a million dollars.

Goals are not absolutes. Since *MFP* doesn't know if your budget is realistic or not, it's also indifferent to how high or low you set the reach/frequency goals. Once you set the goals for national or spot buys, you don't have to go back and change them to continue buying. Goals are planning guidelines, not absolutes.

Reach/Frequency: Although higher reach/frequency may be desirable, avoid jacking up GRPs simply for the sake of higher reach/frequency. What marketers want is brilliant thinking behind the GRPs. Mindless media buying is myopic; corporations will only hire and promote people who learn to create ingenious, strategically driven media plans.

Step 4: National and Spot Contingency
If you have a generous budget, it's a good idea to hold some money back for marketing emergencies. Open the **Budget** screen and change your budget to the amounts shown below:

Total Budget Amount:	$8,000,000	***This $1 million contingency can be used anytime. If you run short, take it out and spend it.**
National Contingency:	500,000*	
Spot Contingency:	500,000*	
Effective Budget:	$7,000,000	

Step 5: Make National media buys for June
Click **[Campaign Settings]** tab and make sure starting month is set for June. At bottom of the screen, your Theoretical National GRPs should read 280. This is simply a "theoretical" goal – an educated "guess" made after MFP multiplies R times F. Put your cursor in the UNITS column. Begin buying the media of your choice for *PF Chang's* – buy until you accumulate 280 GRPs. Normally, you would do a lot of research before choosing media, but for now, make buys that you consider reasonable for your client. Also, as a rule of thumb, *buy a minimum of 20 GRPs in a medium or daypart.*

Avoid chasing reach/frequency with every buy you make. Focus more on strategy and less on pushing reach/frequency higher. Clients (and professors) care most about why you buy and less about cranking GRPs higher. Be true to your strategy and avoid playing the numbers game for games sake.

Step 6: Make Spot buys for June
Check out the Natl + Spot area near the bottom of your screen – note that your total GRP goal for June is 480. You've already bought 280 GRPs in National media. This leaves you with a "theoretical" 200 [AD] Spot GRPs to spend. Buy 200 more GRPs in spot media. Remember that spot market newspapers are different than national. *Newspapers (40% HH Cvg)* is *not* purchased using GRP units. Each unit in this medium equals one insertion. For example, if you type the number 4, you are buying four newspaper insertions that month in all of your spot markets.

Step 7: Monitoring the Budget in June
By now you should have bought a total of 480 GRPs: Your buy includes 280 GRPs in national media and 200 GRPs in spot media for June. Report total dollars you've spent thus far for June in the box below:

Budget Update for June		
Natl + Spot GRP Goal (From Est. Perf. Section)	Total $ Spent-June (From Est. Perf. Section)	Balance Remaining (from $8 Million)

Step 8: Money Goes Fast
You've probably spent about half of your $8 million budget (perhaps over half), and you've only bought June. Actually, $8 million is a very generous budget for a single quarter, and with experience you'll learn ways to stretch the money. Recall that the main objective in this exercise is to challenge you to discover strategies for conserving budget. *Keep in mind that all goals are theoretical, and there is no rule that says you must achieve all goals, or that you must achieve all goals in all months.*

Step 9: News Bulletin! Budget Downsized

You just received a memo from the marketing director. Competitive pressures in *PF Chang's* northeastern region require budget cuts in all other regions. To assist your sister stores, your budget has been cut by 50%. Instead of $8,000,000, your advertising budget is now $4,000,000.

Step 10: Click on Budget and change Total Budget to $4,000,000

There are no absolute "rules" when it comes to strategy, so start thinking creatively.

Your task is to start over in June, and not exceed the $4 million. To conserve budget, you are free to change anything in the case except the Target Demo and the Total Budget, and you cannot advertise longer than three months: June, July and August. There are no other rules – review the case thoroughly, and experiment with different media options.

Step 11: A few tips to get you thinking

• Review the *PF Chang's* case in Exercise 13. Evaluate your client's marketing situation, and consider extreme measures as well as moderate cuts.
• Consider each item in *MFP* and evaluate how you could change it to conserve budget. What about using less expensive dayparts? Would less expensive Ad Types work for this brand? Experiment and find creative ways to save money.

Step 12: Finish up your campaign in July and August

After June, develop your strategy for July and August. You need to address all three months and yet remain inside the $4 million total budget.

Step 13: Print out a Flowchart, your Goals, and staple both print outs to this exercise.

Step 14: Reveal your strategic genius

Alas, few companies will pay you to throw money at marketing problems. There are infinite ways to stretch the budget. List at least eight strategies that you employed.

1. _____
2. _____
3. _____
4. _____
5. _____
6. _____
7. _____
8. _____

CREATING YOUR FIRST MEDIA PLAN USING MEDIA FLIGHT PLAN

Objective: Become proficient using the software tools in Media Flight Plan. Proficiency will result in the creation of an intelligent **National + Spot media plan**.

PREPARATION:

To get the exercise materials , log into the MFP website (www.mediaflightplan.com). Click on **Ground School,** then click on the heading titled **FIRST MEDIA PLAN.** Read the plan outline all the way through.

TIME TO LAUNCH MFP:

1. Click the **Launch MFP** button
2. Under **Campaign Setup**, Click **Target Demo**. Support target decision using the data provided in the *First Media Plan* materials.
3. Click **Campaign Settings** and make decisions on the following:
    Flowchart Titles
    Scope
    Calendar
4. Click **Spot Markets**. Support decisions using data provided in *First Media Plan*.
5. Click **Budget. Decide on budget** using *First Media Plan* data.
6. Click **Goals** to set both National and Spot goals.
7. Click **Ad Types**. Make decisions based on *First Media Plan* data.
8. Make all of your buys using *First Media Plan* as a guide.
9. Click **Year at a Glance** to monitor your budget, reach, and frequency. This tool is your friend and will help keep your budget and R/F goals in check. Learn to use it well
10. Click **Flowchart**. Provide two print outs: First, print the online flowchart. Second, learn to use the **Export to Excel** tool.
11. Click **Monthly Detail.** Print a sample month to see how this works.
12. Click **Market List** to print a list of the markets you've chosen.

This exercise will be considered complete when you turn in a flowchart and any other print outs required by your professor. Your professor may ask for reports other than those listed in the assignment above. Your grade will be based on how intelligently your MFP generated media plan utilizes the *First Media Plan* data. Keep in mind that you have two goals:

1. Achieve proficiency using the tools in Media Flight Plan
2. Create an intelligent National + Spot plan based on the *First Media Plan* data.

NOTE: If you get lost or have trouble using any of the MFP features, refer to the online TUTORIAL found in **Ground School**. You can download or print it if you haven't already.

WRITING SWOT, OBJECTIVES & STRATEGIES: VILLAGE SURF SHOPPE

A 1-2 day case study to test your knowledge of three concepts: SWOT, Media Objectives & Media Strategies

Village Surf Shoppe provides an excellent platform for learning the most intellectually challenging part of the business – organizing and writing the plan. Three chapters in Media Flight Plan are especially relevant to this assignment:

- *Marketing Driven Media Plans*
- *The Art of Writing Media Objectives & Strategies*
- *University Media Plan*

Your goal is to demonstrate that you can apply the principles in these three chapters. Begin with the SWOT – it will test your organizational skills. Next, translate your SWOT into a set of six media objectives. And finally, the most creative part of the assignment: Translate your objectives into strategies – strategies that prove you can think and write imaginatively. Review these chapters thoroughly, especially the case examples in the chapter *Organizing A Media Plan*. Tip: Start early – a first draft on this project will be transparent and obvious to Village Surf's marketing director.

Suggested Point Distribution
- SWOT 20%
- Media Objectives . . 30%
- Media Strategies . . . 50%

Village Surf Shoppe – A Retail Case Study

Since 1969, the Village Surf Shoppe and its manufacturing arm Perfection Surfboards, have been leading players in the surfing business near South Carolina's Grand Strand. Located in Garden City (within the Myrtle Beach retail trade area), Village Surf is an authentic surf shop in the classic 1960's tradition; it is a laid-back surfer hang-out as well as a comfortable place for tourists. Its advertising slogan, "Hardcore since 1969" reflects unwavering loyalty to the serious surfer. It stands in contrast to the uniformly corporate retail environments of national chains like Ron Jon's.

The facility is a simple cinder block structure, hand-painted with beach images. The interior retail space is tightly packed with surfboards, beachwear, and related products. Surfing lessons, camps, and rentals are also important sources of income. Village Surf Shoppe is much more than a place of business, however; it's a gathering place for avid surfers, the primary target market. These hardcore wave-riders often hang out at Village, telling stories and checking out the new boards.

Surfing's New "Inland Market"

Surfing is one of the fastest-growing sports and leisure activities with over 5 million surfers worldwide. Currently, the U.S. is experiencing a surfing boom as demonstrated by new surfing communities in places like New York City and the shores of the Great Lakes. The growing target market for Village Surf Shoppe is men and women, 18-24 with active, adventurous lifestyles. They are also heavy consumers of recorded music and spend considerable time on the Web. Incomes are less than $28,000 annually.

Popular culture has aided the growth of this market. TV programs such as North Shore and Summerland have exposed millions to the lure of surfing. Similarly, films like Blue Crush and MTV's reality show, Surf Girls, have attracted female surfers to the sport. Recent documentaries such as Riding Giants and Step into Liquid are two of the highest grossing DVD rentals in the country. Many surfers get information about surfing products and weather conditions on the Internet and regularly network with other surfers via e-mail, blogs, and chat rooms.

These developments have led to the new inland surfing market. This new market is willing to drive 1-3 hours to the ocean on a regular basis. Today, it's no longer necessary to live in a beach town to be a surfer. For example, for Village Surf Shoppe, inland markets are emerging in Columbia, South Carolina, Charleston, South Carolina, and Charlotte, North Carolina.

Marketing: Past, Present, & Future

Beyond personal selling and word-of-mouth, guerilla marketing has been the chief media vehicle for the store. Village Surf stickers and t-shirts have been enormously successful in achieving product awareness. Stickers and decals can be seen on cars, skateboards, schoolbooks, etc. If you wander through Myrtle Beach and surrounding areas, you'll notice teenagers wearing the classic Village Surf t-shirt. The peak selling period is April through September; sales decline considerably during the winter months.

Event marketing has also been important. The company sponsors surf competitions on a regular basis. Traditional advertising has been limited and sporadic. Occasional publicity is generated in local news outlets and national surf magazines.

Village Surf management feels it is time to take the business to a higher level. Local competition from Waller Bear's, Surf City, and Eternal Wave create the need for new markets. For this reason, the inland market appears to have great potential and will, hopefully, increase sales by 20% in the next three years. About $200,000 has been committed to inland advertising and promotion for the upcoming year.

The Assignment

This first case study assignment is designed to explore the connection between the SWOT analysis and the creation of market-driven media objectives and strategies. Your challenge includes three parts. First, to organize relevant information in the SWOT so that it leads to media objectives designed to solve marketing problems. The objectives and strategies flow out of the SWOT and make up the last two parts of your case.

I. Use the information outlined in this case to write a maximum 2-page "mini" SWOT (i.e., situation analysis: Strengths, Weaknesses, Opportunities, and Threats). For this assignment, organize your paper using the following headings as outlined in the chapter Marketing Driven Media Plans:

        1. Marketing Objectives
        2. Competition
        3. Creative History
        4. Target Audience
        5. Geography
        6. Timing
        7. Media Mix

II. Write a set of six media objectives based on your SWOT analysis. Write one media objective for each of the following as illustrated in the chapter *The Art of Writing Media Objectives & Strategies*.

1. Target Audience & Media Mix
2. Reach – Frequency*
3. Scheduling & Timing
4. Media Budget
5. Geography
6. Sales Promotion

*Make rough estimates for R/F, and don't worry about nailing the "right" reach/frequency numbers. The important objective in this case is to learn to organize and integrate all six objectives.

III. Write a set of six media strategies – one strategy to accompany each of your six objectives. Strategies are ideas that bring the objectives to life. Also, keep in mind that 50% of your score is based on this part of the assignment. In reviewing the Coca-Cola case (in *The Art of Writing Media Objectives & Strategies*), it's obvious that creative strategic thinking is what makes or breaks the brand – the client values strategy more than anything else. Also, keep in mind that this is the marketing intensive part of the assignment. Intelligent marketing is the linchpin to success in business, whichever path you take. Prove you are up to the task by writing a set of six original strategies that pay off your media objectives.

Suggested Length? Strategy is not about quantity; it's all about quality. Look to Coca-Cola and the winning student case study as good models.

Case study sources: Village Surf Shoppe Management, Myrtle Beach, South Carolina. Village Surf Shoppe web site: www.villagesurf.com. Also, 2004 SRDS The Lifestyle Market Analyst.

Case Study Authors: Professor Daniel Stout, University of South Carolina with Professor Dennis Martin, Brigham Young University.

USING DIGITAL MEDIA DATA

In the *Digital Media* chapter, you learned about some of the services, measurements, and techniques used in planning, buying and optimizing digital campaigns. This exercise will give you the opportunity to apply what you know to your client's situation. You will also see how different objectives may change the way you evaluate a campaign.

Your client, Delorme, a leader in GPS, digital mapping and software solutions, has asked you to build a campaign that will build awareness of the brand. Your campaign has been running for about a month now, and it is time to start evaluating performance of the small, but powerful campaign you've designed.

1. The initial goal of the campaign is to build awareness. Click-Through-Rate (CTR) is the most commonly accepted metric to determine the effectiveness of a website at driving brand awareness. While CTR is not directly correlated with driving brand awareness, it is logical that a high CTR (i.e., high number of people clicking per each impression served) indicates that a campaign has a positive impact. Conducting an online brand awareness study would be a better method to establish effectiveness, but your client has limited resources to start and has agreed to use CTR as a means of establishing which websites are doing the best.

The web measurement service you use shows the following delivery and clicks by website for your campaign. Calculate the Click-Through-Rate for each website and add it to the table below:

Website	Delivered Impressions	Clicks	CTR (Click Through Rate)
ESPN.com	2,000,000	7,000	
Eonline	1,000,000	4,000	
Zillow.com	1,500,000	3,000	
AllRecipies.com	500,000	850	
History.com	1,200,000	2,200	
iVillage.com	750,000	2,500	

2. There are two months left in the campaign. In order to improve results, you decide to eliminate two of the websites. Which will you eliminate and why?

3. After the awareness presentation to the client, the GPS division manager is wondering if a different tactic should be used to improve the volume of traffic to the company website. You recommend using Cost-Per-Click (CPC) as a measure of the efficiency of a publisher website at driving traffic to an advertiser website, and warn that your recommendation may well be different from the one you made for awareness.

In your table, you've added the cost of the impressions for each of the websites. Finish the table by completing the calculations for cost per click:

Website	Delivered Impressions	Clicks	Cost of Impressions	CPC (Cost-Per-Click)
ESPN.com	2,000,000	7,000	$30,000	
Eonline	1,000,000	4,000	$15,000	
Zillow.com	1,500,000	3,000	$ 7,500	
AllRecipies.com	500,000	850	$ 3,500	
History.com	1,200,000	2,200	$ 8,400	
iVillage.com	750,000	2,500	$ 3,750	

4. You need to add a 'one-line' description of how to use CPC (i.e. is a high or low CPC desirable) and how that indicates which websites are better. What will you write?

5. When you present to the client, you explain that even though a website may be effective at driving clicks by having a high CTR, different websites may be better when the cost of media is factored in, as when using CPC. With a new campaign objective of increasing traffic to your company website, which two websites do you recommend dropping and why?

6. Your analysis so far has impressed the GPS manager. He mentions he has some extra funds set aside specifically to promote purchase of add-on maps for GPS units from the website, and wants your recommendation as to which websites to run 'map specific' ads. These will run in addition to the awareness advertising that is currently running. You explain that measurement services can provide information on the number of 'actions', such as requesting information, making purchases, or registrations that result from ads shown on publisher sites. Since purchases can be made on the company website, you recommend that the measurement company track 'purchases' as the action you wish to follow. Cost-Per-Action (CPA) is the accepted metric to determine the efficiency of a publisher website at driving website sales.

Will you recommend a high or low CPA? What will your decision indicate?

7. You've received the following sales data by website from your provider. Complete the CPA analysis:

Website	Delivered Impressions	Actions	Cost of Impressions	CPA (Cost-Per-Action)
ESPN.com	2,000,000	7,000	$30,000	
Eonline	1,000,000	4,000	$15,000	
Zillow.com	1,500,000	3,000	$ 7,500	
AllRecipies.com	500,000	850	$ 3,500	
History.com	1,200,000	2,200	$ 8,400	
iVillage.com	750,000	2,500	$ 3,750	

8. Which three websites will you recommend to receive the extra funds, and why?

9. In the table below, indicate with a check which two websites you would eliminate based on each of the CTR, CPC and CPA criteria. Explain why you might want to consider different criteria, instead of say, focusing just on CTR?

Website	CTR	CPC	CPA
ESPN.com			
Eonline			
Zillow.com			
AllRecipies.com			
History.com			
iVillage.com			

10. In digital as in other media, we use indices to indicate the likelihood that our target exhibits specific behaviors online or offline (e.g., watch videos online or visit Pandora). In the Digital Media chapter, you learned about defining targets. Running reports and interpreting them is an important part of the process. The Delorme client has decided to target 18-34 year olds as they are especially active in outdoor activities and make good prospects for their handheld GPS devices.

Your data provider has issued report, but parts were illegible when they came through on the fax machine. You realize that there is sufficient data on the report to fill in the missing data, and decide to do it by hand rather than loose time by having them re-run it. Complete the report by calculating the missing data and indexes. (The target audience for this report is adults 18-34):

Behavior	Total Base Audience	Percent Vertical of Total	Target Audience	Percent Vertical of Target	Index
BASE- 18+ Years Old	181,628,000	100.0	25,416,000	100.0	100
Used Social Media Past 30 Days	139,480,000	76.8	21,650,000	85.2	111
Watch 1-5 video streams on average day	69,669,000	38.4	12,254,000	48.2	
Visit Newspaper site Past 30 Days	58,243,000	32.1	6,244,000	24.6	
Played Gaming Console Past 30 Days	42,890,000	23.6	10,203,000		
Streamed Pandora Past 30 Days	15,743,000		4,751,000		

11. Based on your calculations, which kinds of sites (social media like twitter, facebook; video streaming like YouTube,etc; news sites; gaming sites or streaming audio like Pandora) would you be most likely to recommend?

12. Which kind of site does not perform well against the 18-34 year old target?

13. What does the index for "Streamed Pandora Past 30 days" mean? The index for newspaper sites? Be specific—which direction from average and by how much. (Hint: read the section *Calculating Indexes* in the chapter *Using Indexes to Identify Target Audiences* if you need help)

13. In order to craft a strong digital media plan, digital media objectives must be clearly defined. A common mistake advertisers make is selecting digital media channels without defining a digital media objective. An advertiser can never expect to succeed with a digital media plan if they have not yet decided how to define success.

Given the following digital media objectives, please select the best digital media channel possible (in some cases there may be more than one). HINT: Review the advertising funnel earlier in the chapter as a guide.

Digital Media Objective	Best Digital Media Channels
Drive sales on the website and in-store.	
Build awareness for a new product.	
Drive uses of the store locator on the website	
Encourage customers to advocate on our behalf.	
Increase social media property following (e.g., Facebook, Twitter, Pinterest)	
Drive repeat purchases of current customers.	
Build consideration for a product by increasing engagement with the website.	

MEDIA MODELING EXERCISE

This exercise will use more data from the Politz study mentioned in the chapter reading.

1) As measured by the Politz study in 1953, *Life* magazine has an average audience of 22.1%. Estimate the GRPs, then using basic probability, estimate the reach for each of 6 cumulative issues. Finally, create a frequency distribution for a 3 issue schedule.

a) GRPS (Recall GRPs=average rating x spots):

b) Reach of each of 6 cumulative issues (Hint: Use *and* and *not* to calculate those not exposed at each level, then subtract from 1. Convert to decimals first.):

Issue #	1	2	3	4	5	6
Decimal Cume						
Cume % (x 100)						

c) Use the binomial expansion to build the entire frequency distribution for a 3 issue schedule (Hints: Convert percentages to decimals, recall that 'n' is the total number of issues, and 'k' the level we are looking at each time. Use **E#5** or the '=combin(n,k)' formula in Excel for the number of ways, and **E#6** for the probability). *Carry decimal values to four decimal places.*

# Issues Read (k)	# of Ways $\binom{n}{k}$	Probability	Decimal Result	'x 100' to convert to %
0				
1				
2				
3				
			Total	

Does the sum of all frequency cells total 100% as it should?

d) What is the average frequency (recall average frequency=GRPs/Reach) for this 3 issue schedule?

Exercise 19

2) Combine your 3 issue frequency distribution for *Life* with a two issue schedule for *Look* and estimate the full schedule distribution, GRPs, and average frequency. *Look* has a frequency distribution of 78.06, 15.10, and 6.84 for 0, 1, and 2 exposures respectively. Remember to convert *Look* probabilities to decimals. *Carry cross-multiplication to 4 places.* (Hint: Use the 'decimal result column from problem 1c for the probabilities for *Life* magazine. Don't forget the 'unlabeled' levels 4 and 5!)

	# Issues	Probability	Look Magazine Distribution		
			0	1	2
	# Issues	Probability			
Life Magazine Distribution	0				
	1				
	2				
	3				

Frequency	Proportion	Percent (x 100)
0		
1		
2		
3		
4		
5		
Total		

Does the total still add to 100%?

What is are the total GRPs, reach, and average frequency for this 5 magazine schedule?

3) Estimate the parameters 'a' and 'b' for *Life* magazine using the measured cume values for C1 and C2 from Politz given below. Estimate the frequency distribution using BBD. Plot the data for Politz, BBD, and Probability (use your answers from 1b) on the graph. Which does a better job of estimating cumulative reach compared to Politz?

# *Life* Issues	1	2	3	4	5	6
Cume Reach %	22.1	32.4	39.1	44.0	47.7	50.6

a) Calculate 'a+b' (use **E#17**)

b) Calculate 'a' (use **E#18**)

c) Calculate 'b' (use **E#19**)

d) Use *Microsoft Excel* calculate $\beta(a,b)$ (use **E#20**)

e) Use these values to complete the cumulative reach curve for 6 issues of *Life* (REMEMBER! substitute 'b+n' for 'b' where necessary! Use **E#16** for reach and **E#20** in *Excel* for the beta function):

k	$\beta(a,b+n)$	$\beta(a,b)$	Cumulative Reach Proportion for k issues (Use E#14)	Percent Reach for k issues(x 100)
0				
1				
2				
3				
4				
5				
6				

f) Graph the results for Politz, and your BBD (from 3e) and probability estimates (from 1b)

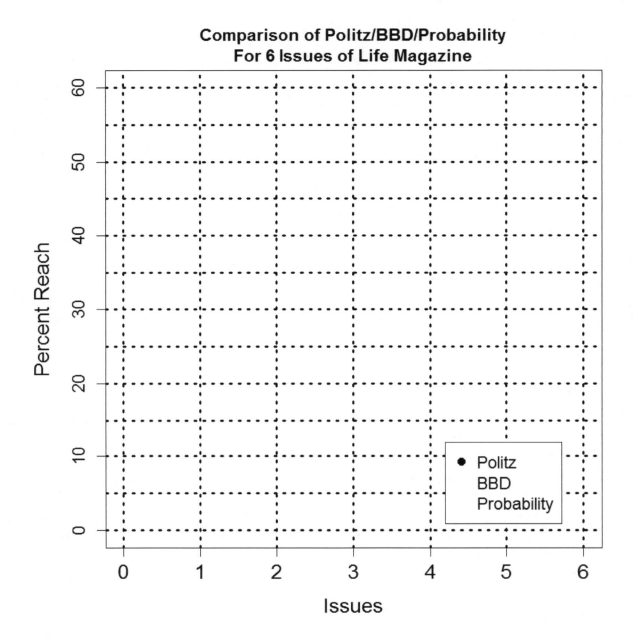

Which is closer to the measured values, BBD or probability?

4) Calculate the frequency distribution, GRPs, reach and average frequency estimates for a 4 issue schedule in *Life* using BBD. *Carry results to 4 decimal places.*

a) Use **E#13** for the frequency distribution. (Hints: REMEMBER to substitute 'a+k' for 'a' and 'b+n-k' for 'b' where necessary! Use **E#20** in Excel)

k	$\binom{n}{k}$	β(a+k,b+n-k)	β(a,b)	Proportion Exposed k times (Use E#13)	Percent Exposed k times (x 100)
0					
1					
2					
3					
4					
				TOTAL	

Does the total of all cell percentages equal 100?

b) How many GRPs are generated by 4 issues of *Life*?

c) What is the reach? (Subtract the 'o' cell percentage from 100)

Does it match the cumulative reach for 4 issues you calculated in 3e? (It should)

d) What is the average frequency for this schedule?

Section III

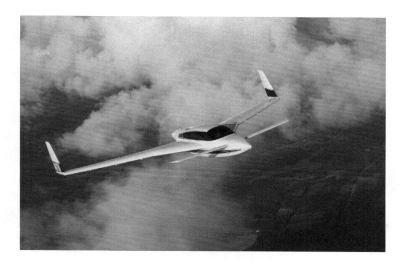

Case Studies

All case studies are online:

1. Go to www.mediaflightplan.com and log in
2. Click **Ground School**
3. Scroll down to **MFP CASE STUDY PACKAGES** and select the case you need.